2nd

BUSINESS AND PROFESSIONAL COMMUNICATION

in the Information Age

John William Haas

HAYDEN
McNEIL

Hayden-McNeil Sustainability

Hayden-McNeil's standard paper stock uses a minimum of 30% post-consumer waste. We offer higher % options by request, including a 100% recycled stock. Additionally, Hayden-McNeil Custom Digital provides authors with the opportunity to convert print products to a digital format. Hayden-McNeil is part of a larger sustainability initiative through Macmillan Higher Ed. Visit http://sustainability.macmillan.com to learn more.

Printed in the United States of America

10 9 8 7 6 5 4 3 2 1

ISBN 978-0-7380-7943-1

Hayden-McNeil Publishing
14903 Pilot Drive
Plymouth, MI 48170
www.hmpublishing.com

HaasJ 7943-1 F15

TABLE OF CONTENTS

Chapter Three

The Process of Communicating and Organizing

■ Unit Two

Chapter Four

The Interviewing Process

Chapter Five

Business Presentations: Preparation

Chapter Six

Business Presentations: Delivery

Chapter Seven

Informative, Persuasive, Group, and Special Occasion Presentations

Chapter Eight

Using Language

■ Unit Three

Chapter Nine

Developing Effective Workplace Relationships

Chapter Ten

Intercultural Communication

Chapter Eleven

Communicating in Teams and Groups

Chapter Twelve

Group Decision Making and Problem Solving

■ Index

SYLLABUS

Instructor		
Office	Mailbox	
Office Phone	Office Hours	Department Phone/Messages 865-974-0696
Email Address		

Course Requirements and Policies

COURSE OVERVIEW

Communication Studies 240 is designed to achieve two broad objectives. First, the course will advance your knowledge of the communication process in business settings. You will accomplish this objective through a combination of oral and written assignments that are designed to prepare you for communication in the workplace. Second, the course is designed to strengthen your skills as a speaker. You will advance your skills through actively participating in a series of individual and group presentation assignments. Following the completion of the course, you will be prepared to build on your understanding of organizational communication so that you may continue to strengthen your business communication skills.

COURSE OBJECTIVES

After completing this course, you should:

1. Possess an understanding of the communication process;

2. Possess an understanding of how to prepare, deliver, and evaluate messages in organizational contexts;

3. Demonstrate an understanding of the ethical responsibilities associated with business communication; and

4. Demonstrate the skillful use of communication in interpersonal, group, and presentation contexts.

REQUIRED TEXT

Business and Professional Communication by John Haas

WEB PAGE RESOURCES

School of Communication Studies
http://www.cci.utk.edu/commstudies/oral

Hodges Library
http://www.lib.utk.edu/instruction/speech210.html

Finding Statistical Information
UT Library
http://www.lib.utk.edu/instruction/statistics.html

Statistical Resources on the Web
http://www.lib.umich.edu/govdocs/statsnew.html

Center for Business and Economic Research (UT)
http://bus.utk.edu/cber/

Databases
http://www.lib.utk.edu/databases/

Business News Sources
Business Week
http://www.businessweek.com/

Wall Street Journal
http://online.wsj.com/home-page

Money Magazine
http://money.cnn.com/

Bloomberg Financial Network
http://www.bloomberg.com/?b=0&Intro=intro3

Forbes
http://www.forbes.com/

Fortune Magazine
http://money.cnn.com/magazines/fortune/

Media and Marketing News

Marketing VOX—The Voice of Online Marketing
http://www.marketingvox.com/

Direct Marketing News
http://www.dmnews.com/

Advertising Age
http://adage.com/index.php

Media Week
http://www.mediaweek.com/mw/index.jsp

Corporate Financial Information and Exchanges

UT Library
http://www.lib.utk.edu/cgi-perl/dbBroker.cgi?subheading=50

New York Stock Exchange
http://www.nyse.com/

NASDAQ
http://www.nasdaq.com/

International Business

CIA—The World Factbook
https://www.cia.gov/library/publications/the-world-factbook/index.html

International Market Research Reports
http://strategis.gc.ca/epic/site/imr-ri2.nsf/en/gr-01000e.html

Trade Data
http://www.ic.gc.ca/epic/site/tdo-dcd.nsf/en/Home

Local Sources

Knox County Government
http://www.knoxcounty.org/

State of Tennessee
http://www.state.tn.us/

Knoxville Chamber Partnership
http://www.knoxvillechamber.com/

Student Responsibilities

In order to achieve the course objectives, you must conform to the following policies:

Communication Studies 240 is not a lecture course. Rather, it is designed as a performance course. Most of your time will be spent interacting with others through presentations and class activities. You are responsible for reading the material assigned for each class.

Class attendance is mandatory. Absences will affect your final grade as follows:

- For M/W/F classes, you are permitted a total of three (3) absences for *any* reason, including sickness, funeral, personal emergency, school-sponsored event, etc. For a T/R class, you are permitted two (2) absences for *any* reason, including sickness, funeral, emergency, school-sponsored event, etc.

- *Each* additional absence, beyond the number permitted, will result in a reduction of your final grade (as determined by your instructor).

- All assignments must be submitted on time. Because major assignments such as presentations and exams are announced well in advance, a makeup will only be allowed in the case of a documented illness or family crisis and with the consent of your instructor.

- It is your responsibility to contact the instructor concerning illnesses or other circumstances that prevent attendance *before* the next scheduled class meeting, or if possible before the absence occurs.

Four broad guidelines have been established for the presentations:

- Presentations must be original and reflect careful preparation. Standards of originality and thorough preparation require that the viewpoint, structure, and style of the presentation be your own, except where specific indebtedness is acknowledged by oral and written citation. The university policy concerning academic integrity will be applied in this course (see page 11 of your Student Handbook, *Hilltopics*).

  University of Tennessee Honor Statement: "An essential feature of the University of Tennessee is a commitment to maintaining an atmosphere of intellectual integrity and academic honesty. As a student of the university, I pledge that I will neither knowingly give nor receive any inappropriate assistance in academic work, thus affirming my own personal commitment to honor and integrity."

- All presentations must be within the boundaries of good judgment and taste. If you are in doubt about what is appropriate, check with your instructor *before* the presentation is delivered.

- You must adhere to all legal statutes governing the community and university. Illegal or hazardous articles or materials (drugs, alcohol, firearms or other weapons, live animals, explosives, etc.) and potentially disruptive or dangerous activities (tuning motorcycle engines, extracting snake venom, cleaning fish, etc.) are *not* permissible in the classroom under the guise of visual aids or demonstrations. If you are unsure whether your visual aid meets these guidelines, contact your instructor in advance for approval.

- You may not jeopardize the safety of any audience member.

Assignment List

The course assignments will be selected by your instructor from the following list:

SELF-INTRODUCTION PRESENTATION

New organization members must be introduced to co-workers. The purpose of this assignment is to introduce you to other members of the organization (i.e., the class) in a brief presentation. Your instructor will determine the length of this presentation. For this assignment, share with the audience information about you that would be appropriate for the workplace and allow you to develop effective workplace relationships.

IMPROMPTU PRESENTATION

Many speaking situations that you encounter in the workplace will be impromptu. That is, you will be required to speak with little or no preparation. Not surprisingly, it is a challenge to represent yourself (and your organization) well in work situations involving impromptu presentations. One of the goals of this class is for you to organize your thoughts and present them clearly. The impromptu speech will give you the best opportunity to think on your feet and recognize the importance of a well-organized message.

INFORMATIVE OR DEMONSTRATION PRESENTATION
Requires presentation outline

Organization members are frequently called upon to inform others about workplace processes or procedures. Choose a work-related topic for this presentation that is informative in nature and includes at least five (5) appropriate sources of information.

PERSUASIVE PRESENTATION
Requires presentation outline

For this assignment, select a topic that involves something that you seek to change (such as a policy or procedure) about your organization. You will prepare and deliver a presentation designed to change or reinforce the attitudes, beliefs, and/or behaviors of the audience regarding the policy or procedure. Include at least five (5) appropriate sources of information.

GROUP/TEAM PRESENTATION
Requires presentation outline

As part of a group, students will prepare a persuasive presentation involving a product or a service. Your instructor will work with you to identify an appropriate product or service-related topic for this assignment. Each group will delegate internal roles in a manner so that the instructor can easily identify each group member's contribution to the project. Include at least five (5) appropriate sources of information for this assignment.

INTERVIEW PROJECT

For this assignment, you must select a person who currently holds a professional position similar to one that you might seek in the future. For example, if you seek to become a marketing manager for a media company, identify a person who currently holds that kind of position. Arrange and conduct an interview with that person, using the sample interview guide located in the interview chapter of this text. Prepare a two-page summary of the interview and provide an evaluation of your performance as the interviewer. Alternatively, your instructor will assign a mock interview to be conducted in class.

RÉSUMÉ/COVER LETTERS PROJECT

You will compose a résumé and cover letter appropriate for use as part of an actual job application process, using factually correct information about the company and yourself.

EXAMINATIONS

Examinations will cover assigned readings and information covered in class. Exams may include multiple-choice, matching, true/false, and short-answer questions.

RESEARCH PARTICIPATION

Each student will have the opportunity to participate in two (2) research projects during the course of the semester. For your participation, you will receive extra credit. This assignment has been developed to support research projects of faculty and graduate students. Your instructor will announce the dates for the research participation.

Please note: If you miss research participation credit, you might not be able to make it up. There is no guarantee that another extra credit opportunity will be offered.

Criteria for Grading Presentations

Communication Studies 240 instructors follow the same guidelines in grading assignments. In general, a C on a presentation means that you have met the minimum requirements for that assignment; a grade of A or B means that you have exceeded the minimum requirements in a significant way; and a grade of D or F means that you have failed to meet two or more of the requirements for the assignment. The average grade for major presentations in this class is a C. In addition, attempting or merely completing a presentation does not guarantee that you pass the assignment. More specific information on grading criteria is provided below.

1. **C = Average, satisfactory work**. To be judged as average and satisfactory, your work must:

    a. Meet all specific requirements for the assignment (length, purpose, organization, sources, delivery, etc.)

    b. Be delivered on the assigned date and within the appropriate time limit

    c. Exhibit sound organization—a clear purpose, adequately supported by main ideas that are easily identified

    d. Be intellectually sound in developing a topic of worth, with adequate and dependable supporting materials

    e. Fulfill any special requirements of the assignment, such as use of three examples of supporting material

    f. Reflect clear, understandable delivery

    g. Be correct in grammar, pronunciation, and articulation

2. **B = Above average work**. To be judged as above average, your work must meet the criteria for a C, as well as the following:

    a. Exhibit skillful use of connectives/transitions

    b. Demonstrate above-average skill in using language, organization, and supporting materials to engage and challenge the audience

    c. Establish genuine rapport and interaction with listeners through style and delivery

    d. Challenge the audience to think, or arouse in listeners a depth of response

3. **A = Superior work**. To be judged superior, your work must meet the criteria for a C and B, as well as the following:

    a. Constitute a genuinely individual contribution to the audience's thinking

    b. Demonstrate exceptional skill in using the communication elements to create audience understanding and acceptance of a complex viewpoint or argument

    c. Illustrate skillful mastery of connectives/transitions and of presentation of ideas

4. **D or F = Below average work**. To be judged below average means that your work is deficient in some or several of the factors required for an average C grade. **Any presentation that is read from notes or lacking the required number of sources cannot be assigned a grade above a C.**

Additional Grading Criteria

Dress Code. On presentation days, all students are expected to dress in business casual clothing. Research is clear on this point: Speaker appearance has a direct impact on audience perceptions of credibility.

Cell Phones and Electronic Devices. Turn *off* your cell phones and electronic devices (e.g., iPod) before the class starts. You will be penalized if your phone rings during a scheduled class meeting. Your instructor will inform you of the penalty for his/her class.

If you have questions about the policies or procedures, it is your responsibility to raise the issue with your instructor. If you are unable to resolve the question with your instructor, you may schedule a meeting with Dr. John Haas, Director of the School of Communication Studies. His office is located in 293 Communications Building.

Unit One will introduce you to contemporary issues in the study and practice of business communication. In this unit, you will also be introduced to two closely related processes: communication and organizing. Key terms in the reading will be identified and questions for discussion are provided to guide you through the material.

CHAPTER 1
- Introduces the reader to business and professional communication in the information age.

CHAPTER 2
- Introduces the reader to the basic communication process that guides interaction.

CHAPTER 3
- Introduces the reader to the major theories that guide our understanding of organizational communication.

UNIT 1

CHAPTER 1

BUSINESS AND PROFESSIONAL COMMUNICATION

Overview

Perhaps no other area of work life is changing more rapidly than the way people communicate in organizations. We are witnessing changes in the way people interact in business and industry on a truly unprecedented scale. For organization members, changes in the way we communicate offer new and innovative ways of working together to achieve individual and organizational goals. However, new ways of communicating are often accompanied by the need to master different skill sets as well as deal with unexpected challenges. In today's business world, a person must be able to interact in a variety of ways involving face-to-face, group, public, and mediated communication. Never before have people needed to possess such a broad array of skills and knowledge in order to be judged a competent communicator.

To become a competent communicator in this rapidly changing work world, you will need to communicate skillfully when you meet face-to-face, when delivering presentations, when working as part of a team, or when exchanging messages through electronic channels such as email, instant messaging, and video-conferencing. A skillful communicator in today's workplace is able to hold an informal conversation with clients while on an elevator, construct persuasive email messages, interact effectively with people from diverse cultures, and communicate so as to achieve goals with supervisors, co-workers, and subordinates.

The idea that people need to communicate effectively in organizations is not new. Communicating in organizational or institutional settings has been a part of the fabric of human society for more than 5,000 years.[1] The task confronting speakers in the information age is to integrate new ways of conveying information with time-tested understandings of effective communication.

In Chapter One, you will learn about:

- The Current State of Business Communication
- Turbulent Business Environments
- Global Competition
- Workplace Diversity
- New Communication Technologies
- Criteria for Ethical Business Communication
  - Ethical Credo
  - Plagiarism

The material in this text is designed to introduce you to communication in a rapidly changing workplace. We seek to increase your understanding of the principles and processes of communicating effectively in organizations. We plan to do this through a combination of speaking, listening, discussion, writing, and reading assignments. The course assignments are designed to build your skills and knowledge of business communication as we progress through the semester. In addition, you will learn by observing others engaged in business presentations. In this section of the course materials, you will view a brief snapshot of the current state of business communication and provide guidelines for communicating ethically in the business world.

Business Communication: The Current State

The current state of business communication may be best described as a state of transformation. Moreover, the end of this transformation is not in sight. From new communication technologies to greater diversity among clients and co-workers to an increasingly competitive global marketplace, business communicators must adapt to a world unimagined just a generation ago. Consider the following hypothetical situation. Imagine that we could transport to today's date a person graduated from college forty years ago. Imagine what this college graduate from the late 1960s would experience as he/she begins to search for a job. For this individual, a personal computer would be something out of science fiction. The Internet did not exist. No one owned a cell phone. Fax machines were not available. Video-conferencing for the average business was not available. When people in organizations interacted in the late 1960s, face-to-face, landline telephone, and letter were the primary modes of communication.

The business environment would also be shockingly different. For example, in the late 1960s the vast majority of people in the United States (approximately 90%) drove a vehicle manufactured by one of the Big Three automakers—General Motors, Ford, and Chrysler. Today, only 40% of U.S. consumers drive vehicles manufactured by the Big Three.[2] Moreover, it is questionable whether the Big Three can survive in their current state. Similar situations may be found in most every segment of business and industry. In the late 1960s, organizations such as IBM embraced a policy of lifetime employment. Few co-workers spoke English as a second language. Most U.S. organizations were focused on competing with companies across town rather than across the globe. Energy costs were stable, with gas prices rising from $.31 a gallon in 1960 to $.34 a gallon in 1968.[3]

The forces that are changing the workplace would make our fictitious traveler from the late 1960s ill-equipped to handle today's business communication. While many forces are at work, four factors have been particularly impactful on business communication: turbulent business environments, global competition, workforce diversity, and new communication technologies.

TURBULENT BUSINESS ENVIRONMENTS

Organizations exist in environments that are made up of customers, regulations, suppliers, competitors, capital, and potential employees. These features of the work world are changing in increasingly rapid and unpredictable ways. From the use of the World Wide Web to communicate with customers to the pressure to embrace "green" policies and practices to frequent mergers and acquisitions, the business world is changing in dramatic fashion. These changes have only been accelerated by the recent downturn in the global economy. In fact, many organizations make clear in company literature or on Web sites that change is a permanent feature of the work world. For example, the mission and vision statement of high-tech companies such as Lockheed-Martin, Dell Computers, and Boeing stress their commitment to change and innovation.[4] Health care organization Humana focuses on the issue of change in its company literature and makes available "white paper" reports on its Web site that deal with the changing business environment.[5] Even nonprofit organizations such as United Way stress that they seek to provide services in a changing business environment.

To meet the demands of a turbulent business environment, communicators must possess the appropriate communication skills. In particular, a turbulent environment requires business communicators to scan or "read" the business environment so as to adapt their messages to changing circumstances. Flexibility and adaptiveness are keys to the skillful use of communication in the business environment that you will enter.

Scanning in Action

Howard Kurtz, the *Washington Post* columnist, made clear in his May 11, 2009 column how he reads the business environment for the print journalism (newspaper) industry. He states, "I have been one of the industry's most fervent optimists, convinced that somehow, some way, newspapers would find a path to survival. But the last few weeks have shaken my belief... The bleak future becomes clear when one paper after another whacks a third or more of its staff... This is not some temporary downturn; these jobs are gone forever."

Clearly, Mr. Kurtz's scanning of the business environment has led him to a negative view of its future. However, could these same events be "read" in different ways? For example, do you read this as the death of an industry or an industry undergoing a profound transition to a new and possibly exciting future? How you read the results of scanning will determine how you frame your messages and how you will seek to influence the way others frame their messages.

GLOBAL COMPETITION

Recently, one company in the eastern part of Tennessee sought to purchase a computer-driven saw for their manufacturing operations. The company, Emco-Williams, manufactures solid surface countertops and requires equipment that can handle large sections of stone during the cutting and shaping process. After receiving several quotes for the machinery, the company settled on a manufacturer from Italy. The purchased equipment arrived approximately five weeks later from Naples. While other manufacturers were available in the U.S., the Italian company offered competitive prices and a speedier delivery date. Emco-Williams needed to upgrade its manufacturing process so as to better compete with solid surface countertops imported from China that are marketed at Lowe's and Home Depot.

This story is repeated countless times worldwide each day. Because of competition from U.S.-based Barnes and Noble and Web-based companies such as Amazon, the New Zealand bookstore chain Whitcoull's has now ventured into online sales and new promotional practices to retain market share.[6] Beef producers in the U.S. must compete with beef producers in Argentina, New Zealand, and Australia for a share of business with McDonald's, the world's largest purchaser of beef. For the first time in 16 years, Harley-Davidson, Inc. has regained the top slot for motorcycle sales in Japan by overtaking domestic producers such as Honda.[7]

Most every product or service is impacted by global competition. Customers increasingly expect to get what they want when they want it. From a communication view, this competition has placed a premium on timely communication and customer service. For example, Harley-Davidson regained the top sales slot in Japan by expanding its network of customer service so as to respond more quickly to customer inquiries. The work environment that you enter will require high-speed, accurate communication with customers and co-workers from a variety of cultures.

WORKFORCE DIVERSITY

Workforce diversity is an increasingly accepted feature of the business environment. What is workforce diversity? Hewlett-Packard, the computer manufacturer, defines workforce diversity as the following:

> Diversity is the existence of many unique individuals in the workplace, marketplace, and community. This includes men and women from different nations, cultures, ethnic groups, generations, backgrounds, skills, abilities, and all the other unique differences that make each of us who we are.
>
> Source: http://www.hp.com/hpinfo/abouthp/diversity/meaning. html

It is not simply high-tech organizations that embrace workforce diversity. Consider the statement from the U.S.-based company PepsiCo:

> In our business, understanding different cultures is a major advantage. In fact, we view diversity as a key to our future. Our brands

appeal to an extraordinarily diverse array of customers. And they are sold by an equally diverse group of retailers.

To truly understand the needs of our customers and consumers —and succeed in the marketplace—PepsiCo must reflect that diversity in our employees, our suppliers and in everything we do.

Offering a workplace where diversity is valued helps us build the top-quality workforce so crucial to our success—by enabling us to attract and retain great people from a wide spectrum of backgrounds.

Source: http://www.pepsico.com/Purpose/Diversity-and-Inclusion/Commitment.html

Business interest in workforce diversity is driven by changes in the pool of labor available to U.S. firms. The U.S. Bureau of Labor Statistics reports that minorities—including Hispanics or Latinos, blacks or African Americans, and Asians—continue to increase their shares of the U.S. labor force. The rates of growth for these groups are projected to be faster than the rate of growth for whites.[8] For example, between 2002 and 2012, the labor force growth rate for Asians is projected to be 51 percent, compared with about 3 percent for whites. Interestingly, organizations outside the U.S. are also encountering a more diverse workforce. For example, more than 200,000 citizens emigrated from Britain in 2006 to countries such as Spain and New Zealand, while British authorities issued more than 160,000 work visas to foreign nationals from places such as India, South Africa, and Australia.

A more diverse workforce increases the challenges associated with communication. Communicating effectively with those from different cultural and ethnic backgrounds requires a wide range of communication skills that involve both verbal and nonverbal messages. In particular, our expectations about what is or is not appropriate to communicate in work-related situations pose real challenges to business communicators.

COMMUNICATION TECHNOLOGIES
New communication technologies have changed the way people do work in organizations. Furthermore, these new technologies continue to enter the marketplace at an increasing rate. Taken together, these technologies share several important features. First, they increase the speed of communication between people in organizations. Second, new technologies offer ways to access people in situations and locations previously unimagined. Third, new technologies allow for almost immediate access to and sharing of information from most any point on Earth. Fourth, new communication technologies have the potential to make existing business models obsolete.

For those just now entering the work world, it is hard to imagine how an office could function without email, the World Wide Web, cell phones, and voice mail. However, these technologies have been part of the way most companies do business for less than twenty years. With the possibility of accessing information and people anywhere there is an Internet connection, the importance of geographical location of employees becomes less important. The diminished importance of geographical location has changed our thinking about where people work and how we can coordinate activities and deliver services. One consequence of new communication technologies is that employees can often work at home, wherever home may be located. For example, Mary Wood, a market research analyst for the Orange County Convention Center located in Orlando, Florida, works out of her home in Atlanta, Georgia. Through a combination of email, video, and phone conferences, she is able to carry out all of her responsibilities. A second consequence is that it is possible to develop "virtual" organizations in which people work and interact entirely through mediated means. While emerging communication technologies offer new opportunities for business, employees are confronted with new communication challenges, such as how to build effective relationships in the virtual world, as well as how to keep pace with ever-changing technology and increasingly unmanageable amounts of information.

As new communication technologies become widely available, however, existing ways of doing business may no longer be profitable. Industries sensitive to the distribution of information ranging from newspapers to telephone manufacturers to survey research firms are finding it difficult to adapt to new ways of gathering and distributing information. For example, a report released by the Centers for Disease Control and Prevention (which conducts health-related survey research via telephone) noted, "In the last six months of 2008, more than one of every five households (20.2%) did not have a landline telephone but did have at least one wireless telephone. Approximately 18.4% of all adults—more than 41 million adults—lived in households with only wireless telephones; 18.7% of all children—nearly 14 million children—lived in households with only wireless telephones."[9] Few, if any, survey research firms are equipped to conduct business through cell phones. Furthermore, others, such as the newspaper industry, have yet to develop a workable business model that will make online versions of newspapers profitable.

Communicating in the Virtual Workplace: The Case of Mary Wood

As noted earlier, Mary is physically located in Atlanta, but works for the Orange County Convention Center located in Orlando. If you were in Mary's position in this virtual workplace, how would you communicate to build a relationship with your supervisor and with your co-workers?

How do we judge effective communication skills in the virtual world? Does an effective communicator in the virtual world use different skills than those in traditional business settings?

Communicating Ethically

While work life is changing in many respects, those who study business communication continue to believe that ethical communication is an inherent part of all business communication.[10] In fact, expectations for ethical business communication are often consistent across cultures. For example, research involving business school students in Singapore, New Zealand, and the U.S. indicated that students generally hold high expectations for business communication behavior.[11]

Simply put, messages have effects. As a business communicator, your messages have the potential to influence the thinking and behaviors of people inside and outside of your organization. In this course, we will expect you to examine closely the ways your messages might influence receivers, as well as the consequences associated with changing the receivers' thoughts and behaviors. Unethical communication means that the speaker does not conform to the values and beliefs about how we should treat others that are part of U.S. business culture. Consider the following:

- When, if ever, is it ethical for a person to mislead others inside the organization? To mislead those outside the organization?

- When, if ever, is it ethical for a person to withhold information from others in the organization? To withhold information from those outside the organization?

- When, if ever, is it ethical for an employee to remain silent when he/she becomes aware that others in the organization are acting illegally and/or unethically?

Ethics are often viewed as a set of values and beliefs that provide guidelines for behaviors and influence judgments as to what is right or wrong. These sets of values and beliefs offer a perspective from which to understand the ethical content of our own and others' behaviors. For many people, the ethical perspective that they operate from may be clear. Consider how we acquire a personal code of ethics. How did our own set of ethics evolve? Some of us would say that they came from a combination of our families, teachers, friends, religion, culture, and society. However, many of the ethical questions you will be confronted with in the work world may involve ethical perspectives that are based on profession or the culture of a particular organization. For example, the computer manufacturer Hewlett-Packard includes the following statement in their published policy regarding business ethics:

> Our values are the foundation of everything we do. We foster an environment that is open and transparent. We encourage employees to report things that don't seem right and continue to develop world-class tools to help employees ask questions and raise values-based, ethical, or compliance concerns.

> Source: http://www.hp.com/hpinfo/globalcitizenship/ethics/

Business communication often involves an attempt to change something about co-workers or clients. The goal of influencing others carries with it a significant responsibility. Cicero once observed that the ideal speaker might be viewed as the good person speaking well. As a speaker, the best ways of ensuring that you are being ethical is to be honest, avoid name-calling and abusive language, be fully prepared so time constraints don't tempt you to plagiarize, and set ethically sound goals in your preparation process.

ETHICAL CREDO

For the purposes of this course, we conform to the credo for ethical communication approved by the National Communication Association (NCA). The NCA position on ethics may be found at http://www.natcom.org/index.asp?bid=13592 and is as follows:

Questions of right and wrong arise whenever people communicate. Ethical communication is fundamental to responsible thinking, decision making, and the development of relationships and communities with and across contexts, cultures, channels, and media. Moreover, ethical communication enhances human worth and dignity by fostering truthfulness, fairness, responsibility, personal integrity, and respect for self and others. We believe that unethical communication threatens the quality of all communication and consequently the well-being of individuals and the society in which we live. Therefore we, the members of the National Communication Association, endorse and are committed to practicing the following principles of ethical communication:

- We advocate truthfulness, accuracy, honesty, and reason as essential to the integrity of communication.

- We endorse freedom of expression, diversity of perspective, and tolerance of dissent to achieve the informed and responsible decision making fundamental to a civil society.

- We strive to understand and respect other communicators before evaluating and responding to their messages.

- We promote access to communication resources and opportunities as necessary to fulfill human potential and contribute to the well-being of families, communities, and society.

- We promote communication climates of caring and mutual understanding that respect the unique needs and characteristics of individual communicators.

- We condemn communication that degrades individuals and humanity through distortion, intimidation, coercion, and violence, and through the expression of intolerance and hatred.

- We are committed to the courageous expression of personal convictions in pursuit of fairness and justice.

- We advocate sharing information, opinions, and feelings when facing significant choices while also respecting privacy and confidentiality.

- We accept responsibility for the short- and long-term consequences for our own communication and expect the same of others.

PLAGIARISM

When you talk about business communication ethics, plagiarism must also be discussed. **Plagiarism** involves using the work of others and representing it as your own. As a speaker, you must give credit to others for their ideas. In fact, you will be evaluated in this course on the basis of whether you cite sources appropriately. At many colleges and universities, you will be asked to become familiar with an honor statement regarding academic integrity. For example, at the University of Tennessee, the following statement regarding plagiarism appears in the student handbook *Hilltopics* (2007):

> Students shall not plagiarize. Plagiarism is using the intellectual property or product of someone else without giving proper credit. The undocumented use of someone else's words or ideas in any medium of communication (unless such information is recognized as common knowledge) is a serious offense, subject to disciplinary action that may include failure in a course and/or dismissal from the university. (p. 11)

Ways to avoid plagiarism include:

- Get an early start on research. Procrastination may tempt you to use information without knowing where it came from or citing it appropriately.

- Keep track of sources while you work on the project rather than trying to locate appropriate citations at the end of the project.

- Cite all information that did not originate from you or that is not common knowledge.

- Cite sources when you quote, paraphrase, or use the ideas of others.

Getting Started with Business Communication

The material in this text is designed to prepare you for the skillful use of communication in the work world. We seek to increase your understanding of the principles and processes of communicating that impact the way people interact in organizations. It is also designed to enhance the development of your own presentation skills. As we begin our journey to prepare for a rapidly changing work world, our vision for business communication is built on the assumption that you must continue to grow as a speaker and expand your knowledge and skill sets in order to be viewed as a competent communicator. If you rely on what you learn as an undergraduate to carry you through your entire business career, it is unlikely that you will experience long-term success. Consider the student from our earlier hypothetical example that we "transported" from the late 1960s to today. If this student from the 1960s did not seek to grow as a speaker and acquire new skill sets, how easy would it be for this person to find a job in today's economy? Thus, one goal we have for this course is to prepare you for the continuous learning that is required for most every career path.

In order to best advance your communication skills and prepare for the future, we have organized the course to maximize your speaking opportunities. You will learn best through frequent opportunities to speak. When you successfully complete the course, you will have a basic understanding of business communication and a clearer understanding of your own speaking strengths and weaknesses, so that you can continue to grow as you transition into the work world.

Specifically, we will expect you to:

1. Develop an understanding of the dynamics of the communication process in business settings, such as speaker-receiver variables, audience analysis, language use, message organization, and delivery;

2. Prepare, deliver, and evaluate presentations;

3. Develop an appreciation for communication in interview, group, and presentation contexts;

4. Develop an appreciation of the importance of personal and ethical responsibility in business communication; and

5. Develop increased skill and confidence in communicating in business settings.

Key Terms

Business environment

Turbulent business environment

Global competition

Workforce diversity

Communication technologies

Ethics

Ethical credo

Plagiarism

Questions for Discussion

• How comfortable are you with change?

• Have you scanned the business environment of the organizations you plan to apply to following graduation? What does your scanning reveal?

• What is communication like in the organizations where you have worked?

• How do you plan to deal with greater diversity in the workplace?

• How will business communication look forty years from today?

ENDNOTES

1. Rawnsley, H.D. (1912). *Notes for the Nile*. Leipzig, Germany: F.A. Brockhaus.

    Gunn, G.B. (1998). *Instruction of Ptah-Hotep and the Instruction of Ke'gemni: The Oldest Books in the World*. New York: Kessinger Publishing.

2. U.S. Department of Commerce, Bureau of Economic Analysis. http://www.bea.gov/industry/index.htm#annual

    Train, E.T., & Winston, C. (2007). Vehicle choice behavior and the declining market share of U.S. automakers. *International Economic Review, 48*, 1469–1496.

3. U.S. Department of Commerce, Bureau of Economic Analysis. http://www.bea.gov/industry/index.htm#annual

4. Lockheed-Martin, http://www.lockheedmartin.com/aboutus/at_a_glance.html

    Dell Computer, http://www.dell.com/content/topics/global.aspx/about_dell/company/main/company?~ck=ln&c=us&l=en&lnki=0&s=corp

    Boeing, http://www.boeing.com/companyoffices/aboutus/

5. Humana, http://www.humana.com/about/company_information/

6. Cheney, G., Christensen, L.T., Zorn, T.E., & Ganesh, S. (2004). Organizational communication in an age of globalization: Issues, reflections, practices. Prospect Heights, IL: Waveland Press.

7. http://query.nytimes.com/gst/fullpage.html?res=9404E3D81F31F934A25757C0A9679C8B63

8. U.S. Bureau of Labor Statistics, http://www.bls.gov/

9. http://www.cdc.gov/nchs/data/nhis/earlyrelease/wireless200905.htm

10. Reinsch, N.L. (1990). Ethics research in business communication: The state of the art. *Journal of Business Communication, 27*, 251–272.

11. Ghosh, B.C., Fullerton, S., & Taylor, D. (1997). Ethics and communication: A cross-cultural study of CEO potential. *Corporate communications, 2,* 130–137.

CHAPTER 2

THE COMMUNICATION PROCESS

Overview

What is communication? When people are asked that question, there tends to be a wide variety of answers. The concept of communication means different things to different people. For some, communication involves messages in the mass media. For others, communication involves interaction between two or more people who seek to achieve a common understanding. For still others, communication involves the physiological processes necessary to produce verbal messages. Given the wide-ranging meanings people assign communication, it is not surprising that it is difficult to settle on a single definition of communication.

Although few words have as many meanings as communication, there is general agreement that a definition of communication includes the following:

- Communication is a process.

- Communication involves the use of symbols.

- Communication involves a sharing or exchanging of meanings.

While general agreement exists on some features of a communication definition, people disagree on other issues that help us to define communication. Perhaps the most important of these issues concerns intention. **Intention** has proven to be a difficult issue to resolve in definitions of communication. For some, communication need not be intentional.[12] Indeed, many believe that one cannot *not* communicate. The implication of this view is that all we do is considered communication. Although many agree with this perspective, others find this view of communication too broad. For many, the intentional production of messages has a quality that separates it from other kinds of human

In Chapter Two,
you will learn about:

- The Communication Process

- Communication Objectives

- Models of Communication

- Communication and Ethics

- Listening Effectively

- Building Source Credibility

behavior. Thinking about communication in this way suggests that individuals are pursuing a goal or set of goals through the intentional use of symbolic behavior when they communicate with others. The implication of this view is that our study of communication is limited to purposeful interaction.

In this course, you will engage in a number of activities that involve purposeful interaction. That is, you will deliver presentations that will be designed to inform, persuade, and entertain. You may engage in interviews or prepare résumés with one or more goals in mind. Therefore, for the purpose of this course, we adopt a working definition of **communication** as the process of intentionally stimulating meaning in the mind of another.

COMMUNICATION OBJECTIVES

If we view communication as intentional, we believe that people in the workplace are pursuing goals when they interact. Viewing communication as goal-directed can help us better understand the communication behavior of others as well as focus our attention on how we are using communication to achieve outcomes. Research suggests that individuals pursue at least three kinds of goals when they communicate with those inside or outside the organization.[13] First, individuals pursue **functional objectives** when they communicate. Functional objectives involve the kinds of uses that we commonly assign to communication. Specifically, functional objectives include:

- To inform

- To persuade

- To entertain

- To coordinate/regulate

- To question

Communication is widely understood as a tool through which functional objectives can be reached. We pursue one or more of these functional objectives when communicating with co-workers or clients. For example, during a company-wide meeting, an effective manager must inform employees about changes that are taking place in the organization before he or she can persuade employees to support the changes.

A second kind of goal that people pursue at work involves **relational objectives**. Whenever we communicate with others, we define how we view the relationship. That is, we define who holds power and authority in the relationship, whether the relationship is viewed as a friendship, a business relationship, a leader-follower relationship, or some other form of relationship. For example, have you ever approached a supervisor to ask for a raise? When you approached your supervisor, did you ask for a raise or did you tell the supervisor that you must be awarded a raise? Your messages make clear how you view your relationship with the other party or parties. In the example involving the raise, your supervisor may have agreed that you deserve a raise, but may be unwilling to acknowledge the kind of relationship in which the boss can be told to award raises. In this case, the supervisor would not agree with the relational objective that you are pursuing (i.e., that you have the greater power/authority in this relationship). People in organizations often communicate ineffectively not because of the functional objectives (to inform, persuade, etc.), but because they define the relationship in a way that is unacceptable to the other party. Consider the following: Why do you think salespeople seek to establish a relationship before they ask the customer to purchase the product? Effective salespeople know that it is harder for a customer to reject a persuasive attempt from a friend than from a stranger.

A third kind of goal that people pursue at work involves **identity management objectives**. When we pursue this kind of objective, we seek to have others view us in the way that we wish. Like actors on a stage, we try to manage the identity that others have of us. Consider the following: When you interview for a job, how do you want the interviewer to view you? If you wish to be viewed in particular ways (e.g., professional, competent, etc.), how do you communicate so that the other party goes along with the identity you are putting forward? If you seek to be viewed as a professional, you must design your messages to manage that identity, which would involve appearance (appropriate dress), responses to questions (level of preparation and competence), and nonverbal behaviors that indicate you understand what is expected of you. Skillful communicators seek to interact in ways that will allow them to manage their identity when dealing with those inside and outside the organization. However, people in organizations often communicate ineffectively not because of functional objectives, but because of identity management objectives. Consider the following: How will you repair the damage done to your identity as a professional if you arrive late for a job interview? What would you say to the interviewer? In situations where one party does not accept the identity that the speaker is putting forward, achieving functional objectives (persuading, informing, etc.) becomes difficult or impossible.

Each time we engage in communication in the workplace, we pursue all of these goals at once. That is, we pursue functional, relational, and identity management goals in all of our communication. Thus, when you attempt to persuade your supervisor to award you a raise, you also seek to manage your identity as a productive employee and communicate that you view the relationship as a business relationship. As a communicator, you must successfully manage all of these objectives in order to achieve your goals. Failing to achieve your relational objectives may very well mean that you will fail to achieve your functional objective to persuade or inform. As you continue through the term, consider how you pursue these goals in the course assignments.

The Case of the Lost Identity

Group assignments are dreaded by many college students. Groups almost always experience conflict because some members do not carry their weight. (In the social sciences, this is known as social loafing.)

In one recent semester, the students assigned to a group experienced considerable conflict that resulted in a failure to achieve identity management objectives. One student named Dean was accused by another student (Amy) of not carrying his weight at a meeting two weeks before the assignment was due. Amy confronted Dean in front of the other group members and said, "You say you care about this assignment but you don't. You say you always pull your weight but you don't. You say you will prepare our visual aids for the presentation but they never appear. I don't care what you say you are, you're just a big talker." In response, Dean said, "Who in the world put you in charge? I don't report to you. You're not the leader of this group. My part will be done, so worry about yourself."

In this case, both parties seek to strip the other of their identity. Until the identity management goals are resolved, it will be difficult for Amy and Dean to work together. How can they both achieve their identity management objectives?

Models of Communication

One way to develop a better understanding of a concept like communication is to construct a visual representation of what happens when communication takes place. A visual representation has the advantage of bringing into focus how different component parts such as a source and a receiver work together. The goal in this section is to separate the communication process into component parts in order to better understand how it works.

Simply put, a model is a simplified version of the real thing. For example, a model car is a simplified version of a real car. It does not include all of the parts of the actual car, but it does provide a visual summary of the key parts: the wheels, the body, the engine, etc. Because many different models could be developed to represent a single car, you should consider what counts as a "good" model. The way that you judge the worth of a model is to evaluate how well the model represents the real thing. In the car example, you would judge a model that includes wheels that move and a hood that can be raised as superior to a model with wheels that do not move and a hood that cannot be raised.

Models can also be helpful in diagnosing why communication is ineffective. Models tell us how the parts of communication work together. They make clear if one thing leads to another, or if the parts are expected to work at the same time.

Although many different models of communication exist, for the purpose of this course we will focus on two models. **The Source Message Channel Receiver** (SMCR) model, also known as the linear model, is one of the oldest and simplest models of communication. It is sometimes called the linear model because it suggests that communication works in linear or straight-line fashion. The model suggests that when communication takes place, several things occur in a specific order. The model is represented as:

SOURCE MESSAGE CHANNEL RECEIVER (SMCR) MODEL

Source → Message → Channel → Receiver

The speaker is considered the **source**. The speaker encodes a **message** that is considered the content of what he or she is attempting to communicate. The **channel** is the particular medium (e.g., face to face, television, radio, newspaper, etc.) that is used by the speaker to convey the message. The **receivers** decode the message and make an interpretation of what the speaker means. Each party in the communication has a single role as either a source or a receiver. The SMCR model has the advantage of being simple and easily understood, but it does have drawbacks. For example, the original version of the SMCR model does not include feedback. Feedback involves the nonverbal or verbal response from receivers that are sent back to a speaker in reaction to a message. In situations where there is little, if any, opportunity for feedback, the SMCR model can provide an adequate representation of what takes place during communication. If you encounter other situations where feedback occurs during a presentation or interview, the SMCR model will not adequately represent what is taking place. In this case, a different model to represent what is happening would be needed.

A second model that is often used to help people understand what happens when communication occurs is called the **transactional model**. The transactional model offers a different way of representing what happens when we communicate. In this model, people engage in a "transaction" by sending and receiving messages simultaneously. During this simultaneous transaction, **interference** (the factors that inhibit the exchange of meaning or impede the message) and **context** (the surrounding environment or situation) impact the encoding and decoding of messages. The transactional model is more complex than the SMCR model in that communicators are doing more. That is, they construct and deliver messages at the same time that they receive and interpret messages. This model suggests that communication is a more complex activity than is represented in the SMCR model.

TRANSACTIONAL MODEL OF COMMUNICATION

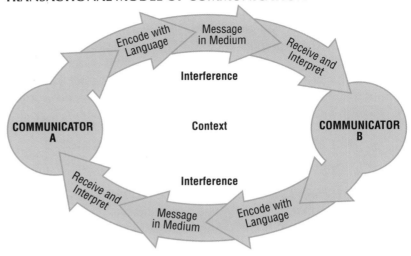

Differences between models. The most important difference between the SMCR model and the transactional model involves the kinds of roles that people play when engaging in business communication. In the SMCR model, a person is either a sender or a receiver. In the transactional model, a person is both sender and receiver. **Feedback** involves the nonverbal or verbal response from receivers that are sent back to a speaker in reaction to a message. In addition, the transactional model adds two new factors: context and interference. This model suggests that context and interference will influence what happens when we communicate. **Context** involves situational factors that influence how communicators interpret their surroundings. The context "frames" the interaction and provides business communicators with a sense of what is expected and what is appropriate. For example, discussing a promotion with your supervisor at a holiday gathering is quite different from discussing a promotion with your supervisor in his or her office. **Interference** (noise) may be thought of as factors that block or inhibit the receipt of a message by receivers. Interference may result from internal causes (e.g., daydreaming) or the result of external causes, such as distractions in the environment (e.g., loud sounds, text messages, movements by others, etc.). Based on this model, effective speakers make use of the context and seek to minimize interference to achieve objectives with listeners.

So, which model best describes what happens when we communicate in business situations? The answer is that it depends on the situation. With the introduction of new communication technologies, an increasing number of business communication events are made available as Webcasts or in other mediated form. In this situation, the speaker occupies the role of the sender and receives little or no feedback from the audience observing the Webcast. The people observing the Webcast occupy the receiver role. It is later that the roles are exchanged. The speaker takes on the role of receiver as responses to the presentation begin to appear in emails or on blogs from audience members.

In many cases, however, the communication takes place in face-to-face settings. In this situation, the speaker sends messages while receiving messages from those in attendance. The nonverbal and verbal messages of the audience provide immediate feedback to the speaker. Thus, when delivering a presentation in front of an audience, all parties in the event are senders and receivers. This setting allows the speaker an opportunity to respond to the messages that he or she is receiving and adapt during the presentation to the audience.

Business Communication vs. Other Communication Contexts

Based on our working definition, all communication may be defined as the process of intentionally stimulating meaning in the mind of another. However, we communicate in many different contexts, such as interpersonal, group, and organizational settings. Each of these contexts differ in terms of the number of people engaging in communication (for example, interpersonal contexts involve two people, group contexts involve three to fifteen people, etc.), the roles that people are expected to play, and a number of other factors. How does business communication differ from other communication contexts?

Business presentations differ from other communication contexts in several ways. The differences include:

- **Roles**. People take on roles in organizations that are different from the roles they take on in other social situations. Roles create expectations for what is appropriate and acceptable to communicate. In fact, those expectations follow us outside of the organization. Have you encountered a teacher at the movies? How would you interact with a current professor if you encountered him/her at a Jimmy Buffett concert?

- **Planning/preparation**. The person delivering a business presentation or participating in an interview generally engages in more planning and preparation for the event than normally occurs in other communication contexts. For example, we do not normally prepare and practice for the conversations that we have with family or friends.

- **Degree of formality**. Presentations, interviews, and meetings tend to be viewed as more formal occasions than our day-to-day conversations.

- **Communication rules**. Many of the rules we use to guide conversation do not apply in business presentations. For example, we expect in conversation that people take turns making contributions to the discussion. In many business meetings or presentation situations, this type of turn-taking would be considered inappropriate.

CULTURAL DIVERSITY

The business world has become increasingly diverse. You will be living and working with people who embrace different religions, values, experiences, and worldviews. Effective speakers recognize that there are different vantage points from which receivers understand their world. Factors such as age, gender, education, race, and ethnicity will have an impact on the values and beliefs embraced by receivers. Culturally insensitive speakers communicate clearly that their vantage point is *the* vantage point from which to understand the world.

You may employ a number of strategies to overcome the challenges associated with a diverse audience. Consider the following:

- **Analyze your audience**. Learn about the cultural similarities and differences in your audience so that you can adapt your message to their vantage points.

- **Reverse the roles**. Would you feel comfortable with a speaker from a different culture if he or she treats your cultural beliefs and values the way you plan to treat their cultural values and beliefs?

- **Avoid ethnocentrism**. Ethnocentrism may be defined as the belief that your worldview is superior to all others. Ethnocentric communicators are offensive to others who do not share that particular worldview.

- **Learn the jargon**. Symbols (e.g., words or phrases, gestures, etc.) are not interpreted the same way across cultures. In fact, what may be viewed in one culture as a very positive symbol may have very negative connotations in a different culture. For example, the hand gesture referred to as the V or victory sign has positive connotations in the United States, but is interpreted as a very offensive gesture in many South American cultures.

Listening Ethically and Effectively

Not only will you be playing the role of a speaker in this class, but you will also be an audience member, which means that you will need to learn how to listen to and evaluate business presentations both ethically and effectively. Listening is a process that involves hearing, evaluating, and responding to spoken messages.[14] From this view, speaking and listening involve two distinct roles in a transactional process. The listening role is the least well understood, because much of what happens when listening occurs internally. That is, listening tends to involve cognitive processes rather than behaviors.

People listen for a variety of reasons, such as the need to gather information, demonstrate empathy, be entertained, be polite, or for the purpose of accepting or rejecting a message. We listen for a combination of these reasons every day. It is important to understand that hearing a message is not the same as listening to a message. Hearing suggests that the receiver was able to detect the sounds directed toward him or her. Listening suggests that the receiver is actually concentrating on understanding the message with the goal of interpreting it accurately.

Research suggests that we spend 75 percent of our waking day listening, which is 50 percent of our entire day.[15] This is more than any other communication skill, including speaking or reading. However, it is the communication skill that we most need to improve. Interestingly, many instructors believe that poor listening is the single largest reason students don't perform as well in class. While covering this chapter, your instructor may ask you to complete a listening self-evaluation to assess your own listening ability.

Often we associate ethics with the speaker rather than the receivers. However, listeners have a responsibility to behave ethically during interviews and business presentations. Effective, ethical listening requires the receiver to be actively engaged when people communicate. The listener shares with the speaker a responsibility for successful communication. When acting in the role of receiver, you are expected to:

- Give the speaker your undivided attention

- Listen with an open mind

- Detect the speaker's objectives (functional, relational, identify management)

- Recognize main ideas and the relationships among ideas

- Detect bias and/or prejudice

- Distinguish between statements of fact and statements of opinion

- Distinguish between emotional and logical arguments

- Employ active listening techniques when appropriate

In addition to bringing about ineffective communication, it is unethical and rude to engage in other activities such as texting or talking during a presentation or group meeting.

CAUSES OF POOR LISTENING

We know that people often experience difficulty with the listening process. A number of **filters** present barriers to effective listening. Specifically, these filters include:

- The setting (heat, light, noise, and time of day)

- Receiver interests

- Receiver values

- Receiver assumptions

- Receiver bias

- Receiver background and experiences

When you consider all of the filters that messages must pass through, it is an amazing accomplishment to listen effectively. Overall, our listening skills are so poor that we must identify the causes so we can set goals to improve. Many of us have different weaknesses when it comes to listening. According to Brownell, the following are reasons we do not listen well. Which one(s) are weaknesses for you?

- **Limited attention span**. The attention span of all humans is limited. However, you can work at increasing your attention span. Attention spans can be increased by consciously not engaging in mental distractions such as reviewing the rest of your work day or thinking about the weekend rather than concentrating on the current message. It could also include not giving into physical distractions such as the temperature of the room or how tired you are.

- **Listening too hard**. This occurs when we listen for every detail instead of trying to grasp the "big picture" conveyed in the presentation.

- **Reserving judgment**. Too often receivers jump to conclusions without giving the speaker or the message a chance.

- **Focusing on delivery and personal appearance**. Instead of paying attention to evidence and the content of the message, receivers too often are distracted by delivery of the message and the speaker's appearance.

GUIDELINES FOR EFFECTIVE LISTENING

Improving your listening skills is often a matter of practice. Just as you would practice a sport or an instrument to get better, you must also practice your listening skills. Not only do you use listening skills more often than any component of the communication process, but your success as a business communicator depends on effective listening. People in organizations who are perceived as the most effective communicators possess the strongest listening skills.[16] The way to improve your listening skills is to set yourself specific goals to improve your listening and monitor your progress in achieving the goals. The following guidelines will aid you in developing effective listening skills:

- Take listening seriously

- Resist distractions

- Do not be diverted by delivery or appearance

- Suspend judgment

- Develop note-taking skills

- Focus your listening for main points and evidence

Developing Communicator Credibility

Your credibility as a communicator will impact how successful you are in achieving your objectives. Overall, people are perceived as credible when they are judged as competent and trustworthy. You can enhance your credibility as a business communicator by doing the following:

- Thoroughly research your topic (be prepared)

- Report accurately on the topic being discussed

- Give proper credit to sources and cite information correctly

- Organize your message

- Anticipate the potential responses to your message

- Pronounce words and identify people correctly

- Dress appropriately

- Arrive on time!

LOOKING THE PART

When you deliver a presentation in this course, you must dress appropriately. Appropriate dress is considered business casual attire. The following items are *unacceptable* to wear when delivering an *assigned*, *scheduled* presentation:

- Shorts

- T-shirts

- Hats or bandanas

- Athletic apparel (jerseys, sweats, etc.)

- Torn or dirty clothing

- Sunglasses on your head or around your neck

- Revealing clothing

The online Human Resources journal offers a clear description of what counts as business casual outside of a university setting:

> Because all casual clothing is not suitable for the office, these guidelines will help you determine what is appropriate to wear to work. Clothing that works well for the beach, yard work, dance clubs, exercise sessions, and sports contests may not be appropriate for a professional appearance at work.
>
> Clothing that reveals too much cleavage, your back, your chest, your feet, your stomach, or your underwear is not appropriate for a place of business, even in a business casual setting.

CHAPTER 2

Even in a business casual work environment, clothing should be pressed and never wrinkled. Torn, dirty, or frayed clothing is unacceptable. All seams must be finished. Any clothing that has words, terms, or pictures that may be offensive to other employees is unacceptable. Clothing that has the company logo is encouraged. Sports team, university, and fashion brand names on clothing are generally acceptable.

Source: http://humanresources.about.com/od/workrelationships/a/dress_code.htm

Research on this point is clear. You will not be viewed as a credible speaker if you do not look the part.

Communication Apprehension

Business presentations are often associated with communication apprehension. **Communication apprehension** may be thought of as the anxiety people experience when they think about or engage in communication. People experience communication apprehension in a variety of contexts or situations, such as interpersonal contexts, group contexts, and presentation contexts. The anxiety that we experience when we think about or engage in business presentations is referred to as **speech anxiety**.

Speech anxiety is a common event. In fact, for many people in the United States, delivering a presentation is their single greatest fear. The anxiety that people experience may be expressed in a number of ways, such as sweaty palms, shaking, rapid breathing, etc. For many people, the anxiety that they feel is very pronounced, and the symptoms of anxiety are more readily observable. For others, presentations bring about a modest level of anxiety.

Keep this thought in mind: A moderate level of anxiety is desirable when delivering presentations. The anxiety that is experienced when delivering a speech is a body's way of preparing you to perform well. The physiological changes that place us in this heightened state tend to make the individual more alert and physically prepared to perform. Regrettably, the body can go too far in preparing a speaker to perform well. When this occurs, the speaker is experiencing a level of apprehension that can negatively impact his or her performance.

Interestingly, there appear to be different kinds of speech anxiety. We can think about speech anxiety as a **trait** or as a **state**. Traits may be thought of as long-term, enduring characteristics that individuals possess. For example, adaptiveness is considered to be a trait that is important to skillful communication. The extent to which a person is able to adapt to changing circumstances tends to be fairly consistent. Thus, the trait view suggests that the level of speech anxiety a person experiences reflects a long-term, enduring quality of that individual. The state view of speech anxiety suggests that anxiousness is brought about by particular situations. From this view a person may feel comfortable talking with peers prior to a presentation. However, once the person begins to deliver a presentation, he or she will begin to experience some measure of apprehension.

The good news is that you can learn to manage speech anxiety regardless of the type of anxiety that you experience. The methods that have been developed to manage speech anxiety are based on different ways of attacking the causes of the anxiety. These methods involve:

- **Self-perceptions**. The goal is to change how the individual perceives himself/herself when delivering presentations. For example, a technique known as visualization is often used to help a person "visualize" a successful speaking experience.

- **Visualization**. Visualization as a method of managing nervousness involves the speaker "placing" himself or herself in a hypothetical presentation situation. Visualization is an activity that must take place prior to the presentation. The goal of this method is to vividly imagine delivering an effective presentation or carrying out an effective interview. Simply put, you imagine yourself performing at a high level in a situation that causes nervousness (in this case, public speaking). Athletes participate in this method to perform better on the court, field, etc. Repeatedly visualizing positive performance does appear to reduce fears of speaking because the positive image begins to replace the negative images involved with presentations. Keep in mind that repeatedly visualizing a negative experience may lead to poor performance. Therefore, it is essential to visualize upcoming speaking experiences in a positive fashion.

- **Competence**. The goal is to reduce apprehension by strengthening the skills of the speaker so that he or she will become more competent at business communication. If anxiety is brought about because the individual does not feel that he/she "knows how to" engage in interviews or business presentations, training designed to bring about effective presentation skills will enable the speaker to manage speech anxiety.

- **Skills training**. By enrolling in this course, you are engaging in skills training. As a method of managing nervousness, training requires the individual to gain additional experience as a speaker. People often experience nervousness because they perceive that they do not possess the skills necessary to perform well. You will begin to experience decreasing levels of nervousness as you build your speaking skills over the course of the semester.

- **Physiology**. The goal is to address the symptoms (increased heart rate, nervous stomach, etc.) of communication apprehension so as to more effectively manage it. This approach involves techniques such as relaxation training, which includes taking deep breaths before your speech.

For further assistance in dealing with speech anxiety, visit the School of Communication Studies Web site listed in your syllabus for additional speech anxiety resources. In summary form, we offer additional tips to manage your nervousness prior to and during the presentation. In addition, the School of Communication Studies will offer workshops during the course of the term on how to deal with communication apprehension. Contact your instructor for more information about the workshops.

PRIOR TO A PRESENTATION

- Think positively!

- Use visualization.

- Don't expect perfection. Expect that you will communicate well despite any occasional mistake.

- To bring about psychological relaxation before moving to the podium, imagine speaking to one person at a time.

- Determine to talk to the audience, not at them.

- Seek to communicate, not perform.

- Get a good night's sleep before the event.

DURING A PRESENTATION

- Do not worry that the audience will readily pick up signs of nervousness. Most of the nervousness that you feel is not visible to the audience.

- Communicate in your normal conversational style.

- Slow your rate of delivery. When speakers become anxious, they often speak at a faster rate, resulting in increased nervousness.

- Remember: The audience does not know what you plan to do during the presentation. Thus, they will be slow to pick up on any mistake. Because they do not know exactly what will happen, you can make adjustments during the speech without jeopardizing your objectives.

Key Terms

Communication

    Intention

    Definition

    Goals

Models of communication

    SMCR

    Transactional

Interference

Context

Feedback

Business/other communication contexts

Cultural diversity

Communication apprehension

Listening

Questions for Discussion

1. What is your definition of communication?

2. What are your communication strengths? Your weaknesses?

3. How do you know when you have achieved your communication goals?

4. How do you know when you have failed to achieve your goals?

ENDNOTES

12. Littlejohn, S.W., & Foss, K. (2005). *Theories of human communication* (8th ed.). Belmont, CA: Thomson-Wadsworth.

13. Berger, C.B. (2002). Goals and knowledge structures in social interaction. In M. Knapp & J. Daly (Eds.), *Handbook of Interpersonal Communication* (3rd ed., pp. 181–212). Thousand Oaks, CA: Sage.

14. Floyd, J.J. (1985). *Listening: A practical approach.* Glenview, IL: McGraw-Hill.

15. Brownell, J. (1996). *Listening: Attitudes, principles, and skills.* Boston: Allyn and Bacon.

16. Haas, J.W., & Arnold, C.A. (1996). The role of listening in co-workers judgments of communication competence. *Journal of Business Communication, 36,* 131–158.

CHAPTER 3

THE PROCESS OF COMMUNICATING AND ORGANIZING

"It is a craftsman who can speak in counsel, for speaking is more difficult than any labor."

—Ptah-Hotep, *The Precepts of Ptah-Hotep* (circa 2,200 B.C.E.)

Overview

In many respects organizations have come to dominate social life. We worship in organizations, are educated, earn a living, recreate, and obtain goods and services through organizations. Because we have lived so much of our lives as participants in organizations, we tend to take for granted how organizations work. Have you ever questioned why an organization is arranged and operated in one form rather than another? Have you considered why people behave as they do in organizations? Exploring possible answers to these questions requires that we consider two processes in which humans engage: communicating and organizing.

Communicating and organizing are two different processes that are closely related. As discussed in Chapter 2, when people communicate they seek to accomplish individual goals. Consistent with this view, when people come together to form and work together in organizations they seek to achieve common objectives. Thus, our interest in organizational communication involves the verbal and nonverbal messages among people who are working together to accomplish one or more goals.

As the quotation at the beginning of this chapter suggests, communicating well in organizations is a challenging task. Because it is widely believed that communication plays a central role in determining whether or not an organization is successful, a variety of different theories have been advanced that seek to explain how communication works in organizations, and how it can be made more effective. To date, there is no single theory that explains all we seek to know about how communication in organizations works. Rather, there are several theories that focus on different parts of the communication process in organizations.

In Chapter Three, you will learn about:

- The Process of Communicating and Organizing

  - Theories of Organizational Communication

  - Communication Channels

  - Organizational Culture

  - Key Terms

  - Questions for Discussion

Our goal in Chapter 3 is not to provide you with a complete list of organizational communication theories. Rather, the goal is to make you aware of the key ideas that guide our thinking about how communication works in organizations, as well as how it can be made effective. The theories that we cover in this chapter will explore how organizational structure, relationships among organization members, relationships among units within an organization, and culture impact the way communication takes place.

Classical Organization Theories

Theories that fall within this group are characterized by a strong focus on organizational structure. Although these theories were introduced around the turn of the twentieth century, they continue to influence our thinking about how communication works in organizations. The people who were conceiving of the ideas on which classical organization theory is based were seeking to establish general principles that could be applied to most all organizations. These general principles involved the way a company should organize, develop standards for job duties and responsibilities, establish lines of authority, and motivate workers.[17]

SCIENTIFIC MANAGEMENT

Scientific management is most closely associated with the work of Frederick Taylor. Taylor questioned why there was so much inefficiency and conflict in the businesses of his day. An engineer by training, Taylor sought to establish principles on how the workplace should be organized so as to maximize the productivity of both employers and employees.[18] He and his contemporaries put forward what they described as the four great underlying principles of management:

- **Develop a true science of work**. This science of work was focused on precisely measuring how a worker should carry out tasks. By precisely measuring how a task should be completed, it would be possible to establish performance expectations. Taylor developed time and motion studies to precisely measure how to carry out tasks and was successful at increasing worker productivity (in some instances, increasing productivity by 400 percent). The science of work was directed, in part, to the communication activities required to carry out job duties. Communication was measured in terms of frequency, timeliness, accuracy, duration, and completeness.

- **Scientifically select and develop employees**. In Taylor's time, workers were often not screened carefully to determine whether they were well suited for a particular job. Taylor argued that employees should be selected through scientific procedures on the basis of their intellectual and physical ability to carry out the job duties and responsibilities. From a communication view, this would mean that jobs requiring strong communication skills would be held by those proven or tested to be effective communicators.

- **Link the science of work to scientifically selected employees.** Taylor sought to hire well-suited employees and train them according to scientific principles to carry out their job duties in the single best way.

- **Establish constant and intimate cooperation of managers and workers.** Taylor believed that if managers and workers followed clearly established principles that most all conflict could be eliminated because all (managers and workers) will be conforming to the same policies.

Successfully implementing Taylor's ideas hinged on the precise measurement of work tasks and the willingness of both workers and managers to be governed by a scientifically designed workplace. His interest in communication was directed toward the efficient transmission of messages. Moreover, these messages generally involved downward communication (messages from supervisors to subordinates). Since workers were hired and promoted on the basis of competence there was believed to be little value in upward communication. Simply put, little would be gained by the more competent people at the "top" of the organization listening to the less competent workers at lower levels in the organization.

BUREAUCRATIC MODEL

Max Weber, the German sociologist, put forward the ideas that have come to be known as the bureaucratic model of organizing.[19] Weber's interest in understanding organizations stemmed from his concern with knowing why people follow commands in organizations. Simply put, why do people do what they are told to do at work? How is authority used to maintain an organization and achieve goals? For Weber, seeking to answer these questions led him to theorize that there are three different ways in which power and authority are made legitimate in organizations.

The first way of exercising authority he labeled **charismatic**. A charismatic form of applying power in an organization stems from the qualities of the leader. The exceptional qualities and communication skills of the leader command the respect and loyalty of others in the organization and set the leader off from followers. As noted in the online version of Harvard Publishing:

> Charisma gives the leader the edge he or she needs to give people a reason to believe in their leadership. Charisma itself is the shine on the apple, but not the apple itself. As behavioral scientists have postulated, the shine often comes from what people want to see; it is a reflection of their own selves. The substance comes from the leader. In sales terms, charisma opens the door, but the leader must close the sale.
>
> Source: http://harvardbusinessonline.hbsp.harvard.edu/b01/en/common/viewFileNavBean.jhtml;jsessionid=4KQXPCEPF3MJCAKRGWDSELQBKE0YIISW?_requestid=86164

CHAPTER 3

Organizations as well as social movements are often the creations of charismatic leaders. For example, Steven Jobs, the creator and two-time CEO of Apple was viewed by many as "A natural Pied Piper in an industry littered with good ideas that have been killed by bad managers."[20] This way of applying power and authority to maintain an organization and achieve goals raises an important question: What happens when the charismatic leader leaves the organization? According to Weber, a charismatic form of organizing is unstable because the basis of authority in the organization is tied to one person. The options for commanding and inspiring others in the organization are limited to the charismatic leader. As a result of its natural instability, this form tends to evolve into either the second or third form as leaders are replaced.

A second form for creating order and authority in a company is based on **precedent and usage**. That is, people in the organization come to expect authority to be applied based on custom. Businesses that are family owned often take on many of the characteristics described by Weber for this form of organizing. According to the U.S. Commerce Department, approximately 80–90 percent of businesses in the United States are family owned or controlled.[21] For these organizations, issues such as succession of leaders/owners, advancement opportunities for nonfamily members, and establishing guidelines for family participation present unique communication and organizing challenges. Weber recognized that communication involving this form of organizing would involve a wider range of topics that would often blend family-related topics with business-related topics.

As a result of the limitations that he felt were inherently a part of other forms of organizing, Weber advanced a third alternative that has come to be known as the **bureaucratic model** of organization. His goal was to develop a system of organizing that would overcome the problems that he associated with both charismatic and traditional forms of organizing. Moreover, he sought to improve the efficiency of an organization. In developing his bureaucratic model, he focused on a process of rational analysis that involved designing an organization to meet specific goals. In Weber's view, an organization should operate like a well-designed machine, with each part performing a clear function. Authority stems from rules and procedures that are linked to a position within the organization (such as sales manager or receptionist) rather than an individual. Authority is then arranged hierarchically in the company with more power and authority at the top of the organization than at the bottom.

This hierarchical arrangement is often illustrated through the use of **organizational charts**. For example, in the chart on the following page the director position has a greater degree of authority associated with it than the CCR Clinical Director or the Deputy Director. Moreover, hiring and promotion in the organization is to be based on competence rather than social influence. Motivation is believed to be the result of monetary incentives rather than social incentives. The organization chart also makes clear channels for communication.

NATIONAL CANCER INSTITUTE ORGAZINATION CHART

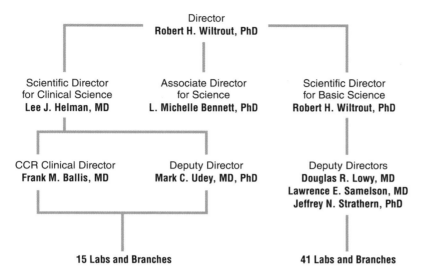

The classical organization theories have a number of implications for communication in organizations. First, the communication focus of classical organization theory was on the formal communication system and its efficiency. Communication was studied and organizations were designed to enhance the formal communication system. Second, the hierarchical arrangement within the organization influences our thinking about the direction of messages. The development of Weber's model led people to think about communication moving in directions. Thus, business operators as well as researchers began to focus on **communication channels**. These channels were conceived as involving upward, downward, and horizontal communication. **Downward communication** is understood as meaning messages being communicated from supervisor to subordinate. **Upward communication** is understood as messages being communicated from subordinate to supervisor. **Horizontal communication** takes place when people at the same level in an organization share messages. Third, informal communication was not a focus of study or interest on the part of management because it was believed to negatively impact organizational efficiency.

When the ideas that fall into the classical organizational theory view were first advanced, they were considered revolutionary. Up to that time, organizations were operated largely in terms of custom and tradition or were based on the vision of a charismatic leader. Classical organization theories brought the first systematic analysis to the practice of organizing and communicating. The ideas behind classical organization theory were responsible for reshaping the workplace and bringing about impressive increases in organizational efficiency. Moreover, these ideas continue to influence our thinking today about how best to organize. However, the emphasis on organizational structure and job tasks offered too narrow a view for many people seeking an understanding of how people work and communicate in organizations.

Human Relations

For those who embrace a Human Relations view, organizations are composed of human beings who bring their interests, goals, and desires to the workplace. People do not simply work in organizations—they are the organization. The recognition that organizations have a social dimension is often associated with what has come to be known as the Human Relations movement. Those who were a part of this movement embraced the same overall objective for organizations as did classical organization theorists. Both groups were interested in creating an effective organization. The people who embraced the Human Relations movement believed that the path to effectiveness involved the social dimensions of the workplace rather than an exclusive focus on tasks or structure. The central idea behind the Human Relations movement was that a happy worker is a productive worker.[22]

Although a considerable number of scholars and practitioners have contributed to this body of work, Elton Mayo and his work as part of the Hawthorne Studies is frequently cited as the founder of the Human Relations movement in the early 1930s. Perhaps his greatest contribution to our understanding of organizing and communicating was his insistence that organizations have an informal component, and that this component was present in every organization. As part of a social system, Mayo argued that individuals would draw benefits from organization membership that had been previously supplied by family or community. The kinds of benefits that Mayo referred to included social support, a sense of belonging, and self-esteem. He further argued that the task of management was to create a system in which people would be able to cooperate together and be motivated by social incentives. Thus, managers (particularly first-line supervisors) were expected to use communication in a new way to develop more effective relationships with workers in order to create a sense of worth in followers and promote worker motivation.

Mayo's thinking about communicating and organizing was shared by a number of scholars and practitioners, including Chester Barnard of AT&T, who authored *Functions of the Executive,* published in 1938. Taken together, this group of scholars/practitioners advanced ideas that were in stark contrast to those advocated by Classical Organizational theorists. The emphasis on relationships and the informal dimensions of the workplace shifted the focus on what it means to be an effective communicator. From the Human Relations perspective, interest shifted from an exclusive focus on timely, accurate, and efficient communication to the use of communication as a tool to develop effective relationships and motivate workers. Moreover, the informal communication network in an organization was recognized, and managers were expected to tap into this network as an important source of information about employee morale and workplace satisfaction. Classical organization theorists believed that informal communication brought about inefficiency and sought to reduce its effects.

Human Relations was widely embraced in U.S. organizations in the late 1940s and throughout the 1950s. The demise of the Human Relations movement stemmed from the difficulty in demonstrating research support for the central idea that a happy worker is a productive worker. Despite this lack of research support, the ideas behind Human Relations continue to influence our thinking about how communicating and organizing should work. Worker satisfaction is believed by many to be an important organizational outcome, even if it does not affect productivity. We continue to believe that effective communication is critical to both relationship development and motivation. In addition, many people in organizations hold out the hope that worker satisfaction will translate into organizational effectiveness. For example, retail giant Best Buy recently embraced a policy that has its roots in the Human Relations movement. As reported by Annie Baxter on Minnesota Public Radio on December 11, 2006:

> In addition to hawking iPods and computers, electronics giant Best Buy is also promoting something with a different kind of gee-whiz factor—job satisfaction. At Best Buy's corporate headquarters in Richfield, the company is incubating a new approach that lets employees work anywhere, anytime. Turnover is down, and productivity is soaring, even though some workers may never get out of their pajamas.

Despite periodic reports like the one above, widespread support for Human Relations was eventually replaced by a view of organizing and communicating designed to overcome the difficulties associated with Human Relations as well as Classical Organization Theory. This attempt to advance our understanding is captured well by a statement from the personnel firm Globoforce:

> What's the difference between a satisfied and an engaged employee? Only everything, argues Globoforce, a Westborough, Massachusetts workforce-solutions Company.
>
> The crux of the difference between the two is discretionary effect, or in laymen's terms, the likelihood that an employee will go the extra mile to get a job done. A satisfied worker probably will not, but an engaged one doesn't think twice before pulling out all of the stops.
>
> Source: http://blogs.eweek.com/careers/content001/working_stiffs/worker_satisfaction_isoverrated.html

Human Resources

The study of organizing and communicating was dominated in the first quarter of the twentieth century by scientific management, and in the second quarter by the Human Relations movement. Much of the second half of the twentieth century has been dominated by what has come to be known as the Human Resources approach to management. The Human Resources approach to organizing builds on many of the ideas of Classical Organization Theory and Human Relations. The overall goal remains the same: organize to bring about high levels of effectiveness. What separates this approach to management from previous approaches is its emphasis on all of the resources (ideas, knowledge, skills, etc.) that each employee brings to the business.

CHAPTER 3

Simply put, organization members do not check their brains at the office door to be retrieved on the way home. Instead, people bring with them to the workplace a pool of ideas about how to address problems and opportunities. In particular, it is believed that greater employee participation can promote organizational effectiveness in decision-making quality. This approach assigns communication a much greater role in the organizing process due to the emphasis on employee input into most all aspects of the business.

In its original form, the Human Resources model also differed from the two previous theories in regard to the way **motivation**, individual **needs**, and **leadership** are conceived. Although monetary incentives are considered the single source of motivation from the Classical Organization Theory perspective and social incentives are the key to motivation in Human Relations, those who embrace the Human Resources approach believe that people are motivated by both. Moreover, ideas about motivation are tied to how we understand needs. The early Human Resource theorists embraced Maslow's hierarchy of needs to account for motivation.[23] Maslow conceived of needs as ranging from basic needs such as food and shelter to higher-order needs involving self-esteem and finally self-actualization. Self-actualization represents the highest-order need and suggests that achieving one's potential is the end state that people seek. From this view, management's role is to organize the workplace so that employees will grow to their fullest stature. Moreover, management should create the kind of work environment where individual goals merge with the company's goals.

Organizations that embrace Human Resources stress opportunities for individual and organizational growth. This focus on individual and organizational achievement is often illustrated in company literature or company Web sites. For example, ExxonMobil states in its recruiting literature:

> ExxonMobil is a dynamic, exciting place to work. We hire exceptional people, and every one of them is empowered to think independently, take initiative, and be innovative.

> Source: http://www.exxonmobil.com/Corporate/careers.aspx

Other organizations, such as The Coca-Cola Company and the Aluminum Company of America (ALCOA) make clear their Human Resources view with recruiting messages such as:

> *Coca-Cola*
> At the Coca-Cola Company we employ people in more than 200 countries around the world... who speak more than 100 languages... a multitude of cultures and geographies and yet we are a local employer. We have a responsibility to enable our people to tap into their full potential; working at their innovative best and representing the diversity of the world we serve.

> Source: http://www.thecoca-colacompany.com/careers/why_work_tccc.html

ALCOA

Alcoa is growing its businesses around the world. To sustain that growth, we need talented, highly motivated people—individuals who want responsibility from day one and the opportunity to make a career with us. In return, we offer a company that values the same things you do, from the environment to family to the community. If you want challenges—and the rewards that go with them—in a dynamic, values-based company that lets you grow and develop, we invite you to learn more.

Source: http://www.alcoa.com/global/en/careers/why_alcoa.asp

The Human Resources view of leadership is guided by the way motivation and needs are conceived. That is, since people are believed to be motivated by monetary and social incentives and pursue needs for self-esteem and self-actualization, the exercise of leadership is guided by a different set of beliefs. Under Classical Organization theory, workers were believed to dislike work and must be closely supervised. Under Human Resources, work is viewed as natural as play and employees are able to exercise self-control in pursuit of individual/organizational goals. McGregor labeled these two views of leadership Theory X (consistent with Classical Organization Theory) and Theory Y (consistent with Human Resources).[24]

While a number of variations of Human Resources have appeared in the business and academic press, this approach to organizing continues to be widely adopted by practitioners. Organizations continue to expect employees to contribute their talent to the company and individuals continue to expect that they will have input into how the company is operated now and into the future.

These three general approaches—Classical Organization Theory, Human Relations, and Human Resources—to organizing and communicating have shaped our thinking about the workings of an organization. Each of these approaches is prescriptive in nature. That is, each seeks to explain more than how organizing and communicating take place. Rather, they lay out how communicating and organizing *should* take place to bring about organizational effectiveness. The debate about which of these theories is best has not been resolved. In fact, other theories such as Systems Theory offer competing views of how to understand communicating and organizing. Nonetheless, much of what we continue to focus on in organizations concerns the themes that are part of the three general approaches we have discussed. The extent to which we should emphasize the rational, structural components or the social components of an organization continues to be debated.

Organizational Culture

Our thinking about communicating and organizing has been influenced by a number of factors, in addition to the three general approaches that we have discussed. Perhaps chief among these factors is organizational culture. **Organizational culture** may be defined as the shared values, beliefs, symbols, and actions of organization members that are passed to succeeding generations of employees. A simpler view was offered by Deal and Kennedy as the way we do things around here.[25] Culture is often used as a metaphor (thinking about or experiencing one thing in terms of another) to draw attention to certain features of a company, such as language use, symbols, and rituals. Thus, in this case we think about an organization as a culture. Organizational culture enthusiasts argue that Dell Computer or First Tennessee Bank have cultures just as Japan or France have cultures. Just as Japan's culture influences the thinking and behavior of the Japanese people, Dell's culture influences the thinking and behavior of the people working for that organization. The interest in culture by both scholars and managers stems from the notion that workers are guided by a set of values and beliefs (i.e., culture). Communication is the "glue" by which the organization's culture (values and beliefs) is created, shared, and sustained.

The study of organizational culture is an attempt to get a handle on the entire organization rather than one of an organization's many parts.[26] From this holistic view, practitioners (i.e., managers) seek to use the concept of culture to reveal why organizations are or are not effective. An organization's culture can be understood as ranging from strong to weak. In an organization with a strong culture, the employees wholeheartedly embrace a set of values and beliefs about the company and its way of doing business. Conversely, in an organization with a diffuse culture, the set of values and beliefs are fragmented and only weakly held by employees. Not surprisingly, a great deal of attention has been devoted to whether culture can be managed in organizations. This interest in managing culture stems from the belief that a company's culture will impact organizational effectiveness. Managing culture will lead company officials to influence the values and beliefs of organization members by managing symbols in the organization. If it can be managed, organizational effectiveness will be impacted by the extent to which employees embrace the company's culture. From this perspective, the role of management is to communicate so as to influence the extent to which employees come to embrace the culture.

Managers seek to manage culture through a variety of means. For example, Deal and Kennedy argued:

> In strong culture companies, managers take the lead in supporting and shaping the culture. We have dubbed these people "symbolic managers," because they spend a lot of time thinking about values, heroes, and rituals of the culture, and because they see their primary job as managing value conflicts that arise in the ebb and flow of daily events.[27]

Managing symbols through communication involves events and activities as well as being strategic about the kinds of interactions that take place with other organization members. For example, universities make use of rituals such as commencement to underscore the value that is placed on acquiring an education. In other instances, managers will make clear what kind of culture they hope to build through publications and Web sites. For example, Google posts this description of its culture on its Web site:

The Google Culture

Though growing rapidly, Google still maintains a small company feel. At the Googleplex headquarters almost everyone eats in the Google café (known as "Charlie's Place"), sitting at whatever table has an opening and enjoying conversations with Googlers from all different departments. Topics range from the trivial to the technical, and whether the discussion is about computer games or encryption or ad serving software, it's not surprising to hear someone say, "That's a product I helped develop before I came to Google."

Google's emphasis on innovation and commitment to cost containment means each employee is a hands-on contributor. There's little in the way of corporate hierarchy and everyone wears several hats. The international Webmaster that creates Google's holiday logos spent a week translating the entire site into Korean. The chief operations engineer is also a licensed neurosurgeon. Because everyone realizes they are an equally important part of Google's success, no one hesitates to skate over a corporate officer during roller hockey.

Google's hiring policy is aggressively non-discriminatory and favors ability over experience. The result is a staff that reflects the global audience the search engine serves. Google has offices around the globe, and Google engineering centers are recruiting local talent in locations from Zurich to Bangalore. Dozens of languages are spoken by Google staffers, from Turkish to Telugu. When not at work, Googlers pursue interests from cross-country cycling to wine tasting, from flying to Frisbee. As Google expands its development team, it continues to look for those who share an obsessive commitment to creating search perfection and having a great time doing it.

Source: http://www.google.com/corporate/culture.html

Based on its statement, what is valued at Google? What kinds of people are likely to be successful in this culture? What kind of communication among employees is valued in this culture?

Summary

Although it is true that each organization has unique features, our discussion in this chapter suggests that there are features common to all businesses. Many of those common features involve communicating and organizing. The theories described in this chapter offer a resource for explaining why we organize and communicate in particular ways. How we explain either process (communicating or organizing) will influence our thinking on what we can expect from the workplace, or how to address issues or problems that we encounter at work.

Key Terms

Classical Organization Theory

Scientific management

Bureaucratic model

Upward communication

Downward communication

Horizontal communication

Human Relations

Human Resources

Motivation

Needs

Leadership

Organizational culture

Questions for Discussion

1. What kinds of communication skills are important in a company that follows Classical Organization Theory?

2. How would those skills differ in an organization that follows Human Relations guidelines? Human Resources guidelines?

3. Describe the culture of the University of Tennessee. What is valued at UT? How do managers/administers use language and rituals to influence culture?

Activity

Talking with someone in a management position is a useful way of gaining knowledge of how organizational communication works and extending your personal network. For this activity, select someone in a management position and schedule a time to meet with him/her to discuss communication in their organization. Try to conduct the interview in a private setting, away from telephones or other distractions.

The questions on the sample interview guide below were developed to help you understand how the theories discussed in this chapter influence the way a manager operates. Based on his/her responses to the following questions, what approach to management does this manager embrace?

MANAGER INTERVIEW ACTIVITY
SAMPLE INTERVIEW GUIDE

1. Describe your organization.
   (What is it like to work here?)

2. Describe your duties and responsibilities.

Transition: I want to speak to you for a few minutes about the goals of your organization.

3. What are the goals of your organization?

4. How are employees made aware of the organization's goals?

5. To what extent do employees share the goals of the organization?

Transition: I want to speak to you for a few minutes about organizational change.

6. How, if at all, has your organization changed in the last three years?

7. How, if at all, have your duties and responsibilities changed in the last three years?

8. How are employees made aware of changes that take place in your company?

9. How much input do employees have in changes made at your company?

10. How will your organization change in the future?

11. How will your duties and responsibilities change in the future?

Transition: I want to speak to you for a few minutes about communication in your organization.

12. In general, how would you describe communication in your organization?

13. What kinds of communication skills does a person need to possess to be successful in your organization?

14. What kinds of communication problems do people encounter in your organization?

Thank the interviewee for his/her time.

ENDNOTES

17. Pugh, D.S., Hickson, D.J., & Hinings, C.R. (1985). *Writers on organizations*. Beverly Hills: Sage.

18. Taylor, F.W. (1947). *Scientific management*. New York: Harper & Row.

19. Gerth, H.H., & Mills, C.W. (1976). From *Max Weber: Essays in sociology*. New York: Oxford University Press.

20. Inc.com. http://www.inc.com/magazine/19991001/13575.html

21. U.S. Census Bureau. http://www.census.gov/econ/overview/mu0200.html

22. Eisenberg, E., Goodall, H., & Trethewey, A. (2007). *Organizational communication: Balancing creativity and constraint* (5th Ed.). Boston: Bedford/St. Martin's.

23. Maslow, A.H. (1954). *Motivation and personality*. New York: Harper-Collins.

24. McGregor, D. (1966). *Leadership and motivation*. Cambridge, MA: MIT Press.

25. Deal, T.E., & Kennedy, A.A. (1982). *Corporate cultures: The rites and rituals of corporate life*. Reading, MA: Addison Wesley.

26. Schein, E.H. (2000). Sense and nonsense about culture and climate. In N. Ashkanasy, C. Wilderom, & M. Peterson (Eds.), *Handbook of organizational culture & climate* (pp. xxiii–xxx). Thousand Oaks, CA: Sage.

27. Deal, T.E., & Kennedy, A.A. (1982). *Corporate cultures: The rites and rituals of corporate life*. Reading, MA: Addison Wesley.

Unit Two will introduce you to basic communication skills in the interview process, as well as preparation and delivery of business presentations.

CHAPTER 4
Introduces the reader to the interview process.

CHAPTER 5
Introduces the reader to the process of preparing for business presentations.

CHAPTER 6
Introduces the reader to the process of delivering business presentations and managing question-answer sessions.

CHAPTER 7
Introduces the reader to informative, persuasive, group, and special occasion presentations.

CHAPTER 8
Introduces the reader to effective language use.

UNIT2

CHAPTER 4

THE INTERVIEWING PROCESS

Overview

Interviews are a common feature of the work world. If you have met with a physician to discuss a medical issue, met with a college recruiter to discuss educational options, or met with a teacher to discuss a grade on an assignment, you have participated in an interview. Interviews offer a unique context in which we may pursue both individual and organizational goals. Although the word interview may conjure up an image involving a job search, we participate in interviews for many different reasons to communicate about a wide range of topics. According to Stewart and Cash, interviews may be defined as a *transactional communication event involving two parties, at least one of whom is pursuing prearranged goals.*[28] Interviews may differ by purpose, but they share many characteristics. These shared interview characteristics include transaction, process, parties, purpose, and questions.

TRANSACTION

As we discussed in Chapter Two, communication can be viewed as a transaction in which the parties involved exchange or share messages. Thus, an interview involves an event during which *both* parties are engaged in interaction. The amount of interaction between the parties is often not equal, and the parties may remain in their roles as interviewer/interviewee or the roles may change as the interview progresses. However, regardless of the level of contribution or role, both parties share responsibility for the success of the interview.

PROCESS

Viewing interviews as a process suggests that they are dynamic and ever-changing. Both parties exchange information, respond to the other party, modify their roles, and adjust to changes in the setting. The outcomes associated with the interview may change the relationship between the two interview parties and modify their knowledge and expectations about future interactions.

PARTIES

Two or more people participate in interviews, but not more than two parties. For example, a job interview may consist of one job applicant and two company officials, or a sales (persuasive) interview may consist of two salespeople and one company official. In each situation, the party composed of two people is acting as one, because they pursue similar objectives and coordinate their interaction when dealing with the other party.

PURPOSE

Interviews provide the context for purposive interaction. That is, at least one of the parties (and often both) approaches this event with clear job-related objectives in mind. In this regard, interviews differ from situations in which two people may be waiting together at a physician's office or at an airport. Interviews involve predetermined, significant objectives rather than informal, unplanned social conversation.

QUESTIONS

Organization members engage in interviews because they offer the opportunity to gather information that is available in no other way. For example, we engage in job interviews in order to gain insight into the candidate's ability to express himself or herself and establish a business relationship. Questions are the principal tool that interview participants can use to gather information or confirm the accuracy of the information that they now possess.

As the parties interact during the interview process, both will seek to achieve relational objectives (as discussed in Chapter Two). Keep in mind that relational objectives are pursued regardless of whether the parties are establishing a new relationship or maintaining an existing relationship. The relational component of the interview process offers insight into why communication is taking on a particular form, how the parties feel about each other, and which party is exercising the greatest degree of control. If the parties have interacted previously, they will devote time in the initial portion of the interview to confirming (or clarifying changes in) the existing relationship. If the parties do not have an existing relationship, they will devote the initial portion of the interview to negotiating a view of the relationship acceptable to both parties. This negotiation is designed to define the relationship, and it is carried out in several ways, such as clarifying how people will be addressed and arranging their physical proximity in the interview setting. Once the parties agree on how to define the relationship, they place limitations on who does the talking and what is appropriate to say. A skillful communicator will interact in ways that are acceptable and fitting with the other party, depending on the nature of their relationship (e.g., intimate, casual, formal, etc.).

The Case of the Relationship Definition

Bill Hardin was a newly minted college graduate who landed a job with a nationally known publication (*Advertising Age*) as an advertising sales representative. He was determined to become the leading salesperson in the company. Hardin completed the sales training provided by the company and started contacting potential clients in order to schedule sales interviews. He was able to schedule several interviews in his first week, and eagerly started preparing for each one.

Hardin's first interview was with John Mitchell, the owner/manager of Doe Anderson Advertising (a large regional advertising agency). Known to his friends as Jack, he has owned and operated Doe Anderson for more than 40 years. He has reached the point of thinking about retirement, but is in good health at age 66. Hardin gathered as much information as possible about John Mitchell and Doe Anderson Advertising in preparation for the sales interview. He went into the interview confident that he was prepared.

Hardin's goal was to persuade John Mitchell to run a series of advertisements about Doe Anderson with a view to moving them beyond a regional market to become a player on the national level. Arriving early for the interview, Hardin was determined to make a good first impression and quickly establish rapport with Mitchell. When Bill was escorted into John Mitchell's office, he started off by saying, "Jack, it's good to meet you. I've heard so many great things about you and Doe Anderson." John Mitchell paused for a moment and replied, "Well, thank you. What is it that you want today?" Hardin was a bit disappointed by what he felt was a less than glowing response to his strong opening statement, but launched into the sales presentation. At the end of the presentation, John Mitchell thanked Hardin for his time and indicated he would be in touch. Hardin left knowing that the interview did not go well, but was confused as to why.

What happened?

Mediated Interviews

Traditionally, interviews tend to take place in face-to-face settings. Changes in communication technology now enable organization members to conduct interviews in mediated form. Initially, interviews in an electronic format involved the use of telephones. Electronic interviews have now been extended to a variety of other mediated formats, including videoconferencing, the Internet, and cell phones. These interview formats offer new opportunities to organization members, but they come at a price. Mediated interviews may offer participants the opportunity to access information or other technologies in ways that are not easily done in face-to-face encounters. Parties that are geographically dispersed can be brought together electronically so that members of both parties may actively participate in the interaction. However, mediated interviews change the way communication

CHAPTER 4

takes place in a host of ways, ranging from nonverbal communication to language use to the establishment of relationships. For example, South Trust Corporation, a large regional bank in the United States, has adopted new software that will enable it to conduct the initial employment screening interview in mediated form through the combined use of telephones and computers.[29] According to *Bank Technology News*, the software works by providing the phone interviewer with a set of questions based on the type of job being discussed. As the job applicant responds, the interviewer uses the software to evaluate answers and calculates one of three recommendations: thumbs up, conditional thumbs up, or thumbs down. Both parties may find that establishing a good relationship in this circumstance will be more difficult. Both parties will find that there are other changes that may impact the outcome of the interview.

Mediated interviews restrict both parties to a limited range of visual message content. That is, we have limited (or no) access to nonverbal messages involving body movement, facial expressions, and eye contact. Even the most advanced videoconferencing technology presents images of the other party in only two dimensions that limit our interpretation of nonverbal communication. Limited access to visual information (e.g., nonverbal cues) has the potential to create misunderstandings. Furthermore, participant satisfaction with electronic interviews is mixed. For example, electronic interviews generally result in less turn-taking because there are fewer interruptions. Fewer interruptions lead to longer turns by both interview parties. Thus, it is more difficult to interact freely and naturally. On the other hand, many people like being able to engage in other tasks during the interview (such as responding to a text message) and not disrupt the flow of the conversation. Overall, organization members appear willing to participate in electronic interviews but prefer face-to-face settings.

Interview Preparation

Simply put, preparation is the key to effective interviewing. Without proper preparation, successful interview outcomes will be the product of chance, not design. Most (but not all) of the interviews organization members participate in will allow both parties some opportunity to prepare. Interview preparation begins with the **goals** of both the interviewer and interviewee for the interview. Specifically, what do the parties seek to accomplish? The goals of the parties determine how to prepare for the interview. If the parties are not clear on their objectives, the outcomes associated with the interview will likely not satisfy either party. However, be aware that the goals of one or both parties may need to be modified during the course of the interview. In this type of circumstance, one or both parties must reevaluate what can be accomplished during the interview. For example, if during the course of a persuasive interview (such as a sales interview) it becomes clear that the interviewee (the customer) is not prepared to make a decision today to accept or reject the persuasive appeal, the interviewer (the salesperson) will likely modify his or her objective to gather information about when the decision will be made.

Following the selection of goals, the **topics** that are addressed in support of the goals should be identified. For example, in an employment interview, the interviewer settles on the goal of gathering information to identify the most qualified applicant for the position. In order to achieve this objective, several topics (education, previous work experience, etc.) need to be explored through a set of questions.

Interview Strategy

The interviewer is the party initiating the interview, and it is the interviewer who tends to determine the overall interview strategy. In general, interview strategies can take one of two forms: **directive** or **nondirective**. These strategies are often described as falling on a continuum ranging from directive interviews (sometimes referred to as highly scheduled interviews) on one end to nondirective interviews (or nonscheduled interviews) at the opposite end. The goal in using a directive strategy is to bring about a highly structured, controlled interview. In an interview that is based on a directive strategy, the interviewer will come prepared to the interview with a list of questions arranged in a predetermined order. Each interviewee will be presented with an identical set of questions that are asked with the exact same wording. Interviewees are expected to do most of the talking and be prepared for the topics that are likely to be discussed. For interviews in which this strategy is used, the interviewer exercises control over most all aspects of the interview process. The initial employment interview often involves a directive interview strategy on the part of the interviewer. Because all interviewees are asked the same set of questions, it is easier to compare and contrast the responses of the candidates for the position.

Not surprisingly, a nondirective (or nonscheduled) interview strategy is in many ways the opposite of a directive strategy. Interviewers that make use of this strategy prepare few, if any, questions in advance. Rather, the interviewer has a list of topics that he/she wishes to discuss. However, there need not be a particular order to the topics, and the interviewee will have greater control over the pace and structure of the interview. This type of strategy is often used in the final employment interview or in situations that require the interview participants to broadly explore a topic. For example, an interviewer using a nondirective strategy may begin this type of interview with the request, "I would like for you to share with me in the next 30 minutes how you would attract new business to our company." In his or her response, the interviewee will determine the topics and the order in which they will be discussed.

Between the two ends of this interview strategy continuum (directive and nondirective), interviewers may blend features of the directive and nondirective strategies. The amount of structure the interviewer imposes on the interview process determines where along the continuum the interview strategy falls. The use of this type of "blended" strategy (sometimes referred to as a moderately scheduled interview) by the interviewer allows greater freedom than the directive strategy concerning the questions asked of the interviewee and opportunities to probe into unexpected or unusual responses. Thus, the interviewer does not use a single predetermined set of questions that are asked in precisely the same fashion. Rather, the interviewer makes use of both a set of questions and a topical outline to structure the interview.

Questions—Selecting and Sequencing

We commonly ask questions in day-to-day situations. However, we seldom use questions with as much precision or prior planning as the parties do during the interview process. Because we seek to achieve a variety of goals during the course of an interview (e.g., inform, persuade, gather information, etc.), it is expected that at least one (and generally both) of the parties prepares questions designed to achieve job-related objectives. In this section, we will review the kinds of questions that are appropriate for an interview and examine how interview questions should be used. According to Stewart and Cash, interview questions range between three essential characteristics:

- Open-ended vs. close-ended

- Primary vs. probing

- Neutral vs. leading

OPEN-ENDED VS. CLOSE-ENDED

Simply put, an open-ended question cannot be answered with a single word or phrase. An open-ended question offers the respondent flexibility in deciding how to answer the other party. For example, during an employment interview, an interviewer may ask a question such as, "Tell me what you learned in your major that will make a difference in how well you perform at this company." This question places few restrictions on the content or length of the interviewee's response. Answering this question adequately will require the interviewee to provide a broad response rather than answering with a word or phrase. In contrast to an open-ended question, a close-ended question restricts the possible responses of the other party. A close-ended question is used when the questioner is seeking specific information or if the respondent is asked to select one answer from a set of responses. Most often, the possible responses are reduced to a single word or phrase. For example, an interviewer during an employment interview may ask, "What was your grade point average?" To answer this question beyond a short phrase is inappropriate and would likely not even be recorded by the interviewer. In other instances, the respondent may be presented with a list of possible response options. For example, during a sales interview, one party may ask the other party, "When you consider the purchase of a car, are you most concerned with safety, fuel-efficiency, or cargo capacity?" Note that in this example, the potential responses remain restricted.

Both types of questions have advantages and disadvantages. Topics can be more fully explored using open-ended questions, since respondents have few, if any, restrictions on how they might reply. This type of question is more time-consuming to use, and you may gather information that is not relevant to the interview objectives.

The interviewer must not allow the interviewee to stray too far from the topic being discussed. In contrast, close-ended questions allow the interviewer to gather large amounts of information in a relatively short time. However, there is little, if any, opportunity for respondents to explain or more fully describe their views on the topic. Moreover, the person asking the questions must be very clear on what he or she is seeking in order to make effective use of this type of question. For example, if an organization is clear on the skills and knowledge necessary to perform a job, then it would be possible to construct close-ended questions designed to gather information from job applicants about their skill and knowledge level. However, if this is a newly created position and the skills and knowledge necessary for success are somewhat unclear, constructing closed-ended questions designed to gain insight into the interviewee's knowledge and skills that are relevant to the job will be difficult.

PRIMARY VS. PROBING

A primary question is prepared in advance and is tied directly to the interview objectives. For example, during an employment interview an applicant may be asked, "Why should we hire you?" In contrast, a probing question results from a response to a primary question. In our example from an employment interview, a candidate was asked why he or she should be hired. If the response to that question was interesting, unexpected, or incomplete, it should then be followed with a probing question, as in the following example:

Primary Question: "Why should we hire you?"

Response: "You should hire me because I will increase sales by 50% over the next twelve months."

Probing Question: "That's quite an increase. Tell me how you would increase sales by 50% in the next year."

As suggested by this example, a probing question (sometimes identified as a follow-up question) is designed to gather additional information in connection with the previous response. This type of question may be open-ended or close-ended.

Effective primary questions are the result of preparation. However, probing questions are difficult to prepare in advance of the interview. Effective probing questions spring from skillful listening and the recognition that more information is needed to fully answer the question.

NEUTRAL VS. LEADING

Neutral questions do not lead the respondent to answer the question in any one particular way. That is, the respondent is not given any explicit or implicit clues about how to respond. For example, during an employment interview, an applicant may be asked the following neutral question: "Describe your internship experiences with CBA Recording Company." In contrast, a leading question suggests to the respondent how he or she should answer the question. In a variation

CHAPTER 4

of the previous question, an applicant may be asked, "You learned a great deal during your internship at CBA, didn't you?" In this question, the respondent is led to the answer that learning did take place in this internship. The suggested response may be made clear verbally, as in the previous example, or it may take the form of nonverbal gestures or other nonverbal cues, such as the tone, pitch, and vocal emphasis.

Not surprisingly, leading questions should be avoided in most all interviews simply because the response may not accurately represent what a person thinks or feels. Leading questions are sometimes used in certain types of interviews (e.g., sales interviews), but tend not be used in other types of interviews (e.g., employment interviews). To be used well, the person asking a leading question must be clear on why he or she is using it and how to evaluate the response. People in a range of professions involving health care delivery, law, education, and social work do make use of leading questions during the course of interviews. Moreover, questions can range from mildly leading to loaded. Questions that are mildly leading provide clues to the respondent about what would be deemed an acceptable answer. If the respondent does not have strong feelings about the question, he or she will often offer the other party the answer they seek. For example, it is likely you would readily agree to a leading question in an employment interview such as, "I hope it's okay that we meet in the conference room rather than my office." However, **loaded questions** dictate what counts as the correct answer. Such questions often include the use of words or phrases that evaluate others or are emotionally charged. Such questions leave the interviewee with few, if any, options for responding directly to the question. Consider the following questions:

MILDLY LEADING	LOADED
How do you feel about the use of Facebook at work?	Do you use Facebook like those slackers in the office down the hall?
Have you tried drugs?	Most good employees don't use drugs. When was the last time you tried drugs?
How do you feel about the company monitoring the way we use the Internet at work?	Don't you feel that Big Brother watching our Internet use violates the Constitution?

Mildly leading questions can help an interviewer if used skillfully to (tactfully) remind people of policies and expectations in the workplace. However, loaded questions should be avoided unless the person asking the question has thought through the reason for its use.

QUESTION SEQUENCE

Most all interviews involve the use of more than a single question. Thus, it becomes necessary to put the questions in some order. Sequencing questions is useful in several different ways. First, the interviewer can more readily determine if this set of questions in this order will enable him or her to achieve the interview objectives. Second, it forces the interviewer to organize his or her ideas in advance of the interview. Third, it makes the interview predictable for the interviewee. That is, the interviewee has some way of determining the direction of the interview and the order of the topics that will be discussed. Although business communicators sequence questions in a number of different ways, four methods are widely used in the workplace: tunnel, funnel, inverted funnel, and hourglass. The names for these methods are suggestive of how broad or narrow the sequence of questions will be in each of the four patterns.

Tunnel Sequence

In some interview situations the questions prepared may all be equally narrow or broad. This set of questions is often arranged in a **tunnel sequence**. In a situation in which one party has prepared a string of questions that are similar in breadth, the tunnel sequence is the appropriate arrangement. This arrangement works well even if a variety of topics are covered in the discussion. This type of sequence is used most often in interviews in which the goal is to gather information rather than persuade or evaluate (e.g., medical interviews, orientation interviews, etc.). For example, during a campus visit, a prospective student may ask an admissions officer the following questions:

I am interested in applying to this university. Would you share with me:

- What are classes like?
- What are the dorms like?
- What kinds of social activities are available to students?
- What kinds of majors are available?
- What kinds of support services are offered?

Each of the questions in this sequence is equally broad, even though they cover several different topic areas.

Funnel Sequence

As the name suggests, the **funnel sequence** involves a question arrangement that begins with broad-based questions that are followed by questions with a narrower focus. This is perhaps the most commonly used pattern for ordering questions in an interview. This sequence works well because the initial questions "prime the pump" for the questions that follow. That is, the interviewer starts by having the interviewee think broadly about a topic prior to focusing on some narrower aspect of the topic. For example, in an employment interview, the interviewer may use the following sequence of questions:

- Describe for me how your background and experiences have prepared you for this job.

- Let's focus now on your educational background. Describe for me how your education has prepared you for the position.

- The position that we are discussing today requires strong oral communication skills. Tell me about how your coursework impacted your communication skills.

- Did you have the opportunity to deliver presentations?

- Did you deliver sales presentations?

In this brief example, you can see how the topics become increasingly narrow in the question sequence. Moreover, notice that as the questions unfold, the interviewer changes from open-ended questions to close-ended questions.

Inverted Funnel Sequence

The **inverted funnel sequence** reverses the ordering of the questions as described in the funnel sequence. When using the inverted pattern of questions, the interviewer begins with narrow, close-ended questions and eventually changes to broad, open-ended questions. This pattern is not as easy to use as the funnel sequence, because it is often more difficult for people to transition their thinking from narrow topics to broad-based topics. The following questions illustrate the ordering of the inverted funnel question sequence from the employment interview:

- I noticed on your application materials that you completed a course in business and professional communication. Did you deliver sales presentations in that course?

- Did you have the opportunity to deliver other presentations in that course?

- The position that we are discussing today requires strong oral communication skills. Tell me about how your coursework impacted your communication skills.

- Let's focus now on your educational background. Describe for me how your education has prepared you for the position.

- Describe for me how your background and experiences have prepared you for this job.

Consider both the funnel and inverted funnel question sequence. Which sequence is easier for you to deal with as an interviewee? Which would be easier for you to deal with as an interviewer? For many people, the funnel sequence is easier to manage because of the ease associated with moving from a general topic to a specific aspect of the general topic. However, both have the advantage of providing a clear direction for the interaction during the interview.

Hourglass Sequence

The **hourglass sequence** combines features of both the funnel and inverted funnel sequence. Using this pattern, the parties may begin with broad questions and proceed to more narrow questions. However, the broadness of the topics can be expanded as topics warrant a change in direction. Using our funnel sequence employment interview example, an interviewer can extend the questions by asking close-ended questions about the applicant's major, followed by more open-ended questions about possible career paths.

Not surprisingly, there are variations for each of the question sequence patterns reviewed in this chapter. As you gain experience with interviewing, you will find it easier to modify a pattern so as to better meet your objectives.

THE HOURGLASS SEQUENCE

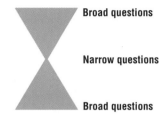

Broad questions

Narrow questions

Broad questions

Conducting the Interview

Although organization members participate in a variety of types of interviews to achieve different kinds of objectives, there are three general components that apply to most all interviews. Our discussion of the component parts to an interview will follow in chronological order and include the following:

- The opening of the interview

- The body of the interview

- The interview closing

INTERVIEW OPENING

In general, interview openings serve to establish rapport between the parties, preview the interview, and identify any special constraints (e.g., time limits, etc.) that will impact the interview. **Establishing rapport** involves the creation of a willing, receptive communication climate between the two parties. Both parties will feel comfortable sharing views with the other party about the topic(s) to be covered in the interview. If rapport is not established in the opening, one or both parties may be guarded about the information they decide to share. In this situation, it becomes more difficult for either party to achieve their objectives.

When the parties do not have an existing relationship, establishing rapport will be aided by preparing for the interview. You will find it easier to create a willing, receptive climate if you are familiar with the other party and their background. Familiarity with the other party will allow you to do what we frequently do when establishing a relationship: point to commonalities. When the parties have one or more things in common (hometown, mutual friends, mutual interests, etc.), they find it easier to begin to build a relationship. Conversely, knowing little or nothing about the other party will make it difficult to become acquainted. The following case provides an example of how preparation aided in the establishment of rapport between the two parties.

<table>
<tr><td>

The Case of the Volunteer Building Alabama Rapport:

A True Story

Rachel Tegano, a former Communication Studies major at UT, was in her final college semester and actively involved in a job search. One position she applied for was with a large media firm located in Birmingham, Alabama. Rachel prepared for the interview by researching the company, its competitors, and the person conducting the interview (Brad Culpepper). Her preparation revealed that they had a number of common interests, including college football.

Rachel was greeted by Brad when she arrived for the interview. After they exchanged greetings, Brad opened the interview by saying that they were impressed with her application materials, but that she had less work experience than they preferred. From her research, Rachel knew that Brad was an avid Alabama football fan, so she responded by saying, "I feel like Jay Barker must have felt his freshman year when he just wanted a chance to play. A lot of folks didn't believe in him, but he went on to win 35 games and a national championship during his career. I'm like Jay; I just want a chance to prove myself." Not expecting this response, Brad sat back and reconsidered her suitability for the job. "OK," he responded, "You made it clear that you've done your homework. Let's talk about the job."

</td></tr>
</table>

Establishing rapport does not guarantee that both parties will achieve their objectives. However, not establishing rapport will make it difficult or impossible for both parties to reach their goals.

The **interview preview** serves two important functions. First, the party initiating the interview generally begins with a statement of purpose. This statement can be delivered in rather informal terms, such as when a student initiates an advising interview with the statement, "I stopped by today to talk with you about my coursework for next semester and about graduate school possibilities." In other types of interviews such as the disciplinary interview, the statement of purpose will likely be delivered in a formal, precise manner. Second, the party initiating the interview provides an orientation statement that summarizes the topics to be discussed. In many interviews (e.g., an employment interview), there is little opportunity to negotiate over the topics to be discussed. In other types of interviews (e.g., sales interviews), it is common for both parties to negotiate to agreement during the interview preview.

BODY OF THE INTERVIEW

The body of the interview is devoted to asking and answering the questions that were prepared by one or both parties. As discussed, the body of the interview ranges from highly structured interaction with a precisely worded list of questions (directive strategy) to a loosely structured discussion designed to broadly address the interview topic (nondirective strategy).

INTERVIEW CLOSING

The closing of the interview serves several functions. First, any unanswered questions may again be addressed with the goal of gathering the necessary information. Second, the outcome of the interview should be summarized in order that both parties come away from the interview with similar understandings. This summary statement tends to be made by the party initiating the interview. Third, the parties should identify what, if any, follow-up actions need to be taken as a result of the interview. Fourth, the parties should seek to reinforce the relationship that they have established.

Types of Interviews

Because people have a variety of communication needs in the workplace that involve gathering information, influencing others, or confirming existing understandings, many different types of interviews are used in organizations. It is not our goal to review all of the types of interviews that are used in business and industry. Rather, you will review several of the most commonly used types of interviews and examine their unique preparation and participation characteristics. For the purpose of this course, we will sample the following types of interviews:

- Employment interviews

- Performance interviews

- Disciplinary interviews

EMPLOYMENT INTERVIEWS

Often referred to as the selection interview, the employment interview is widely used in most all types of organizations to identify and select individuals for new/vacant positions, or for the purpose of promoting an individual to a position of greater responsibility. Both parties have a great deal at stake in this interview. For the employer, there is pressure to recruit the best-qualified person for the position who will make a contribution to the organization. For the applicant, career aspirations may or may not be fulfilled as a result of the interview.

This type of interview is initiated and controlled by the party representing the organization. Although both parties are expected to prepare for this type of interview, the preparation process varies considerably between the interviewer and the interviewee. If carried out effectively, the employment interview process involves a great deal of time and expense for both parties. The employment interview process is carried out in a series of steps that begin with the recruitment and conclude with the employment interviews.

THE RECRUITMENT PROCESS

Although the level of formality may vary, employers follow predictable patterns when recruiting for and conducting interviews. The recruitment process begins with a determination of the job duties and responsibilities that will be assigned to the new employee. In large-scale organizations, this process is often handled through a

CHAPTER 4

human resources department according to the organization's hiring procedures. In smaller-scale organizations, this process may unfold in a less formal way, with the owner/operator working with a clear sense of the tasks that must be carried out by a new employee. Regardless of the level of formality, once the employer is clear on job duties and responsibilities, the bona fide occupational qualifications (BFOQs) can be established. BFOQs refer to the skills and qualifications that a person must possess in order to perform the job. The skills and qualifications generally involve level of education (e.g., college degree), previous work experience, and relevant skill sets (e.g., working knowledge of software programs).

After BFOQs have been identified, the organization will begin the process of recruiting applicants for the position. In general, organizations tend to recruit for positions in the following fashion. First, can the organization fill the position from within? For example, a current intern or part-time employee may be considered for the position. Second, the organization will rely on referrals from current employees. Do any current employees know of a qualified candidate? Third, if no internal candidates or referrals are available, the organization will take one of three routes: it will use current employees to recruit qualified candidates at universities or other appropriate institutions, it will hire an agency to recruit qualified candidates, or the organization will advertise the position through newspapers or other outlets such as Monster.com.

As the recruitment process generates applications, the organization will begin to screen the applications on the basis of the BFOQs that were identified earlier. Applications will be judged against the BFOQs and grouped in a more or less formal fashion as highly qualified, qualified, and not qualified. The organization will seek to interview those candidates deemed most qualified.

For the interviewee, the lesson should be that the majority of jobs that are available are not advertised. In fact, many jobs that are advertised in newspapers or other print/online media are hard to fill and hard to keep filled. These jobs may be highly stressful or unattractive for other reasons. Thus, many organizations tend to approach entry-level positions in terms of a recruitment strategy rather than in terms of a retention strategy. Armed with this knowledge, the interviewee should devote considerable time and effort to networking in order to gain access to information about the jobs that are available, rather than relying on the jobs that are advertised.

While the employer engages in a recruitment process, the interviewee engages in a job search process. This process involves the development of a résumé and cover letters, networking, and submitting applications. In conjunction with UT's Career Services Office, a packet of information is available at http://career.utk.edu/resources.php describing how to prepare for this process as a UT student, as well as how to interact during the interview. The packet includes sample résumés and cover letters, as well as information about the programs offered by Career Services.

The Employment Interview

The employment interview process generally involves a series of interviews. The initial interview provides the interviewer the opportunity to compare those identified as highly qualified. In general, interviewers employ a directive interview strategy when conducting this initial interview and carry out the tasks previously described in the opening, body, and closing of an interview.

The key to effective performance for the interviewee in the series of employment interviews is preparation. In fact, there is no substitute for preparation. Preparation on the part of the interviewee should include the following:

- Researching the company, its products, and services

- Researching its competitors

- Researching similar positions (duties and responsibilities, compensation, etc.)

- Researching the interviewer

Preparation involves knowing about yourself: your skills sets, knowledge, and previous experience. You must be able to relate information about yourself to potential employers. At the end of this chapter is a list of questions that are often asked of interviewees during the course of an employment interview. After reviewing the questions, consider: Are you prepared to answer these questions at this moment? Thus, you should realize the importance of preparation for this interview.

Additional employment interview tips including the following:

- First impressions count, so make sure to dress appropriately (pressed clothing and polished shoes)

- Shake hands firmly

- Smile

- Convey interest and enthusiasm

- Follow up with a thank-you note a.s.a.p.

In addition to employment interviews, organizations make use of many other kinds of interviews. Two important kinds of interviews include the **performance interview** and the **disciplinary interview**. Both of these types of interviews are conducted in terms of the principles discussed earlier in the chapter. However, they differ in terms of purpose. Performance interviews are designed to provide employees with feedback concerning their job performance, and offer guidance in terms of how to improve performance. This interview provides the setting in which supervisors and subordinates can set performance objectives for the employee over the course of the performance appraisal period. In contrast, the goal of a disciplinary interview is to improve the performance of the employee. The goal is *not* to punish. Unless the employee is to be dismissed by the organization, the discussion should center on changing the behaviors that violated the organization's rules.

CHAPTER 4

Key Terms

Interview process

Elements of interviews

Parties

Mediated interviews

Interview structure

Types of interviews

Directive and nondirective strategies

Question types

Activity

Review the following interview questions and consider how you would answer:

- How would you describe yourself?

- What are your long-range and short-range goals and objectives?

- What do you see yourself doing five years from now?

- What do you want to do in life?

- How do you plan to achieve your career goals?

- What are the most important rewards you expect in your career?

- What do you expect to be earning in five years?

- Why did you choose this career?

- Tell me about your views on working with other people.

- How would you evaluate your ability to deal with conflict?

- Have you ever had difficulty with a supervisor? How did you resolve the conflict?

- What's more important to you—the work itself or how much you're paid?

- What do you consider to be your greatest strengths and weaknesses?

- How would a good friend describe you?

- Describe the best job you've ever had.

- Describe the best supervisor you've ever had.

- What would your last boss say about your work performance?

- What motivates you to go the extra mile on a project or job?

- Why should I hire you?

- What makes you qualified for this position?

- How do you determine or evaluate success?

- What do you think it takes to be successful in a company like ours?

- In what ways do you think you can make a contribution to our company?

- What are the attributes of a good leader?

- Describe the workload in your current (or most recent) job.

- Which is more important: creativity or efficiency? Why?

- What two or three accomplishments have given you the most satisfaction? Why?

- If you were hiring a job-seeker for this position, what qualities would you look for?

- Do you have plans for continued study? An advanced degree?

- In what kind of work environment are you most comfortable?

- How do you work under pressure?

- What's one of the hardest decisions you've ever had to make?

- How well do you adapt to new situations?

- Why did you decide to seek a position in this company?

- What can you tell us about our company?

- What interests you about our products?

- What do you know about our competitors?

- What two or three things are most important to you in your job?

- What criteria are you using to evaluate the company for which you hope to work?

- Do you have a geographic preference? Why?

- Are you willing to relocate?

- Are you willing to travel for the job?

- What major problem have you encountered, and how did you deal with it?

- What have you learned from your mistakes?

- What have you accomplished that shows your initiative and willingness to work?

CHAPTER 4

ENDNOTES

28. Stewart, C.J., & Cash, W.B. (2008). *Interviewing: Principles and practices*. Boston, MA: McGraw-Hill.

29. http://www.americanbanker.com/btn.html

CHAPTER 5

BUSINESS PRESENTATIONS: PREPARATION

Overview

One of the most important communication skills necessary for job success involves the ability to prepare and deliver effective business presentations. As with interviews, effective presentations hinge on preparation. Most all experts agree that preparation is the single most important factor in determining whether you will deliver an effective presentation. Far too many people view preparation in terms of simply developing a speaking outline or constructing visual aids. Effective preparation involves much more. In fact, companies that offer communications skills training to Fortune 500 companies such as Productive Training Services, located in Ann Arbor, Michigan, believe that:

> Far too many presentations begin with planning and preparing for the slides and the content instead of preparing the presenter for the audience. Ask yourself…what's more important?…that I connect with my slides and look good?…or that I connect with my audience and help them by adding value?
>
> Source: http://www.productivetraining.com/pages/Home.htm

The goal of Chapter Five is to guide you through the presentation preparation process. That process begins with the speaker identifying his or her goals for the presentation. Once the speaker is clear on the desired objectives, the next step involves analyzing the audience.

General Purpose

The general purpose is the broad-based goal of a presentation and is usually made clear to the speaker when he or she is invited or assigned to deliver the presentation. The three general purposes of a presentation are to inform, persuade, and entertain. As you may recall, these general objectives fall into the category of goals referred to as

In Chapter Five, you will learn about:

- Differences between Audience-Centeredness and Egocentrism

- Audience Analysis

- Analyzing the Presentation Setting

- Adapting to Feedback During the Presentation

- Organizing Your Presentation

- Five Patterns of Organization

- The Use of Connectives

- Four Components of an Introduction

- Three Components of a Conclusion

- Differences between a Speaking Outline and a Preparation Outline

functional objectives in Chapter Two. Keep in mind that speakers are often confronted with situations in which they must pursue two or three general objectives. For example, when delivering a persuasive speech to an audience with little or no knowledge of the topic, the speaker will find it necessary to inform the audience about the topic, as well as persuade them to accept a particular viewpoint.

Specific Purpose

The specific purpose is a single phrase that focuses on only one aspect of your topic. It should state precisely what you hope to accomplish in the presentation. The specific purpose should be stated in such a way that the goal is observable and measurable. For example, if your specific purpose is to persuade each audience member to donate $100 to the Red Cross, it is relatively easy to observe or measure the extent to which you achieved your objective. Moreover, the specific purpose statement is useful because it forces you to zero in on one aspect of a broader topic. If the topic is health insurance and your general purpose is to inform, the specific purpose puts into precise language exactly what you wish to accomplish.

It is often useful to write a specific purpose statement before you begin preparing your presentation. Writing out the specific purpose statement will aid you by keeping the focus on the presentation objective. If the specific purpose is not clear, you have no guide for what to prepare or how to deliver the presentation. The following examples of specific purpose statements make clear what each speaker seeks to accomplish. Notice that the examples begin with a general purpose.

- To inform my audience about the five major steps in administering CPR.

- To persuade my audience to formally consider my funding proposal for the 2009 fiscal year.

- To inform an audience composed of new employees about the health and retirement benefits offered by the company.

SPECIFIC PURPOSE GUIDELINES
The following guidelines will aid you when writing specific purpose statements:

- The topic and specific purpose must meet the requirements of the assignment. Some topics, such as those involving a process, tend to be better suited to informative presentations than persuasive. Similarly, topics that involve some degree of controversy, such as environmental policies, seem better suited to persuasive presentations.

- Your purpose must be sufficiently narrow so that it can be achieved in the time allotted. Avoid the common mistake of developing specific purpose statements that require more than the allotted time to achieve. Far too often students recognize late in the preparation process that they seek to accomplish more than can be achieved in the time allotted.

- It must be relevant to the audience. Specifically, what do they need or want to learn about the topic based on their knowledge and interest level?

- It must not be trivial. Ask yourself, is this information worth knowing?

- It must not be too technical for the audience. Do not choose a purpose that is too specialized for your audience to readily understand in the time allotted.

THESIS OR CENTRAL IDEA

The thesis or central idea of a presentation is a concise, one-sentence statement of what the presentation is about. It explains the content of the presentation by summarizing the main points. The main points divide the content by categorizing the information into a particular organizational pattern. That organizational pattern is generally shared with the audience during the introduction. The goal of sharing this information with the audience is to preview the main points. Because of this, the central idea in a presentation is what a thesis statement is to a paper.

Writing the central idea will be the most challenging step in the process so far. You will not be able to develop the central idea for the presentation until the research on the topic is complete. Without knowing the information available on the topic, it would be difficult or impossible to develop the main points. Thus, the main points of the presentation will emerge from the information you gather during preparation. When you write the central idea, avoid the mistake of making it overly complex (as many students do). Use the following sequence below when preparing your own central idea.

Topic to Central Idea: Sequential Order
- *Topic*: Obesity

- *General Purpose*: To inform

- *Specific Purpose*: To inform my audience of the three major causes of obesity

- *Central Idea*: The three major causes of obesity are genetic predisposition, lack of exercise, and poor eating habits

Think about the stages of this process as beginning broad and becoming more specific, as represented in this funnel.

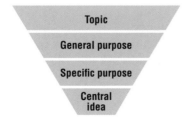

CHAPTER 5

ANALYZING THE AUDIENCE

Audience analysis is an important part of presentation preparation, as well as delivery. In this course you will be expected to adapt your message to a specific group (i.e., your classmates). This practice of adapting messages to the audience should continue after you complete this course. In fact, every presentation you deliver should be adapted to a specific audience.

Audience analysis involves gathering information about the audience in terms of their attitudes, demographic characteristics, level of interest, and knowledge of the topic. You will make use of this information to prepare for the presentation as well as to adapt your message during the presentation.

Audience-Centeredness

One way to understand how business communicators approach presentation preparation and delivery is in terms of egocentrism and audience-centeredness. **Egocentrism** suggests that the speaker simply expresses his or her views that reflect his/her own values, beliefs, and experiences, regardless of the nature of the audience. In effect, this means I'm going to say what I want to say, the way I want to say it. Effective speakers recognize that this is an ineffective way to prepare to communicate with an audience. Receivers understand messages in terms of their values, beliefs, and experiences. The self-centered speaker runs the risk of speaking about a topic in terms that receivers cannot relate to or understand.

In addition, effective speakers understand that members of the audience are also egocentric. Members of the audience understand messages in terms of their own values, beliefs, and experiences, regardless of the speaker's values and beliefs. Since audience members think in their own terms, effective speakers include the kind of information that receivers can relate to and understand.

In order to be viewed as an effective business communicator, you must embrace an audience-centered view of presentations. **Audience-centeredness** means that your messages are adapted to the needs, values, and beliefs of the receivers. This does *not* mean that your goals are determined exclusively by the audience. Rather, it means that the messages that you develop are designed to achieve your objectives in terms that are relevant to the values, beliefs, and experiences of receivers. Thus, a marketing representative for Dell Computer must adapt presentations to each audience but the objective remains the same: persuade the audience to buy Dell computers.

Preparing for Your Audience

Learning about your audience is best done by asking questions about them. Specifically, you should ask the following:

- Who will be in the audience?

- Why are they here?

- What is their knowledge and interest in the topic? In my product/service?

- What attitude(s) do they hold toward the topic, product/service, and me?

- How have they responded to presentations in the past about similar topics, similar products/services, and with similar speakers?

- How do I locate information about my audience?

Who will be in the audience? Determining the audience composition will involve the use of demographic information. **Demographic variables** are qualities or characteristics that can be used to segment or divide the population into groups. Demographic variables that speakers commonly seek information about include age, gender, race, ethnic background, socioeconomic status, and group membership. The possible list of demographic factors is extensive, so it will be important to use sound judgment as to the list of factors that you examine. For example, when preparing for a presentation in this course, the kind of demographic variables that can be used to divide up the audience members would include major, class standing, and gender. However, this kind of demographic information will not be relevant for other audiences. It would not make sense to segment a group of engineers at a professional association meeting on the basis of the same demographic variables (major, class standing, and gender).

Effective communicators realize that all audience members do not respond the same way to a message. In part, different responses to a presentation are the result of demographic factors. Gathering demographic information prior to the presentation will assist you in two important ways. First, you will be able to gather more precisely the information necessary to achieve your goals with that particular audience. The information needed to support your objectives when delivering a presentation to your classmates will be different than the information needed to achieve the same objectives in a presentation to professors. Second, you will be better able to anticipate the possible objections audience members may have to your goals. For example, a professional presentation designed to persuade a local government commission to accept a site selection proposal for a landfill may receive a different response from local officials who have constituents living near the proposed site than from officials who represent voters far from the proposed site.

Why are they here? People attend presentations for different reasons. The people in the audience may be attending the presentation as part of their job duties, they may be required to attend, or they may receive some benefit from attending. Answering the question of why people will attend the presentation is necessary to prepare adequately. The information needed to support your objectives in a presentation delivered to a group of new employees required to attend an orientation session will be different from the information needed to support a presentation with the same objective that is delivered to a group of senior executives.

CHAPTER 5

What is their level of knowledge and interest in the topic? Audience members will have different levels of knowledge about and interest in your topic. Knowledgeable, well-informed audience members will require the speaker to make use of different kinds of information to achieve his or her objectives than less knowledgeable, less well-informed audiences. Similarly, the level of interest audience members have in the topic should influence the kind of material that you include, as well as the kind of material that you exclude from the presentation.

What attitudes do they hold toward the topic? An **attitude** may be thought of as a predisposition or evaluation toward someone or something. For example, what is your attitude toward iPods? Mildly positive? Highly negative? People's attitudes vary in intensity and may range from a highly positive to a highly negative predisposition toward someone or something in their world. Moreover, the audience may be united or they may be divided in terms of the attitudes that they hold. It is commonly recognized that attitudes can influence behavior. You can be certain that audience attitudes will play a central role in whether you achieve the presentation objectives. The audience will hold attitudes about several different features of the speaking event: audience members will hold attitudes toward the topic and purpose of the presentation. The audience will also hold attitudes toward the person making the presentation, the company he/she represents, other members of the audience, and the setting for the presentation.

Answering the question about attitudes will provide you with direction for how to prepare the presentation. If the audience holds a negative attitude toward you or your company, what kind of information will you need to gather to achieve your objective(s)? The information that you will need to gather to support your speaking objectives with an audience who holds a positive attitude toward the topic will be different from the kind of information necessary to achieve your objective with an audience who holds a negative attitude toward the topic. With the second group, you need to gather information designed to reinforce existing attitudes. With the first group, you need to gather information designed to bring about attitude change.

How have they responded in the past? In this course, you will have the opportunity to observe how audience members respond to speakers. What were speakers saying or doing to evoke a strong reaction (positive or negative) from the audience? What were speakers saying or doing when they generated little, if any, response from the audience? You will not always have the opportunity to view how an audience outside of class reacts to other speakers, but you should make use of this information when it is available.

How do I locate information about my audience? You can gather information about your audience from a variety sources. These sources include the following:

- Conducting library research to determine how groups similar to this audience (based on demographic characteristics) view your topic. At the following URL, you will find a wide range of business-related information that is readily available at the UT library: http://www.lib.utk.edu/cgi-perl/dbBroker.cgi?subheading=19

- Contacting professional associations (e.g., Chamber of Commerce, associations of professionals in a field such as the American Medical Association, American Bar Association, etc.) for relevant information. Most all professions ranging from event planners to attorneys to engineers maintain one or more professional associations. Most associations gather information from members that, if available, will give you insight into attitudes and interests of audience members. For example, at the following link to the American Medical Association, you will find information concerning an AMA agenda (described as the collective voice of physicians) and advocacy efforts on behalf of its members: http://www.ama-assn.org/

- Gathering information from the individuals or groups responsible for arranging the event. To whom are they promoting the event? Who received invitations? Who do they expect to attend? How do they think the audience will respond?

- Conducting research or drawing from previous research involving these (or similar) audience members. For your presentations in this course, it will benefit you to learn the audience's knowledge level, interest level, and attitudes toward your topic. This is relatively easy to do in a classroom setting, but may not be as practical in other settings.

PREPARING FOR THE SETTING

Because the setting impacts the presentation, consider how to adapt your message to the setting so as to achieve your objectives. When preparing the presentation, consider the following about the setting:

- **The presentation location**. Speaking opportunities and challenges vary considerably based on the location of the presentation. For example, a conference room location presents a speaker with a different set of opportunities and challenges than a manager's office with limited seating capacity. Simply put, know the location.

- **The physical layout of the room**. The room layout will influence how the speaker establishes the kind of relationship he or she is seeking with the audience. If appropriate, make use of a lectern (podium) and locate it in front of the room so that you will be the focus of attention. In addition, the layout influences the kinds of visual aids a speaker selects for a presentation, because visual aids must be visible to all audience members.

- **Potential distractions**. Possible distractions such as a loud ventilation system or noise coming from adjacent rooms should be considered when preparing for a presentation. Moreover, other factors such as extremes in temperature will impact the attention span of the audience. Prior to the presentation, determine whether the room temperature can be adjusted. If not, be prepared to adjust your presentation based on the impact of room temperature.

CHAPTER 5

- **The time of the presentation**. If you have taken an 8:00 a.m. class, you realize that audience members are not always motivated to listen to the speaker because of the time of day. If possible, select the time for the presentation that you feel audience members will be most receptive to your message. If that is not possible, adapt your message accordingly to the time for the presentation.

- **The audio-visual equipment**. A problem that is increasingly encountered by speakers concerns audio-visual equipment. Too often speakers using presentation software such as PowerPoint find that their equipment, flash drives, or cables are not compatible with the technology available at the location for the presentation. Whenever possible, conduct a test run on the equipment at the facility where the presentation will be delivered to determine system compatibility. Do not assume that your computer, memory devices, or cables are compatible with the technology available at the location for the presentation. A second strategy to avoid audio-visual problems is to bring your own equipment. For example, extension agents at UT bring to the presentation location all of the equipment needed for a PowerPoint presentation, including laptop computers, projectors, extension cords, power strips, and adapters for two-prong wall outlets. If your success hinges on audio-visual equipment that works, learn what the setting has available for speakers.

ADAPTING TO AUDIENCE FEEDBACK

In addition to the time and effort devoted to audience analysis during preparation, it is equally important to continue the analysis process during the presentation. Even well-prepared speakers can be surprised by a range of factors, from unexpected guests in the audience to breaking news stories about your topic to unexpected or disinterested responses on the part of the audience. In fact, speakers often see confused or inquisitive looks on the faces of the listeners. When this occurs, effective speakers retrace their steps and clarify or elaborate on their message, instead of ignoring the nonverbal feedback.

The confidence to make changes in mid-presentation will be strongly influenced by your level of preparation. Knowing the material gives you the confidence to be flexible with the presentation outline, omit or add information, rearrange the order of information, or make unexpected use of stories and anecdotes. However, adapting successfully to feedback requires practice. As your career unfolds, continue to work at strengthening your skill in adapting to audience members.

Adapting during the presentation requires that you accurately diagnose the feedback provided by the audience. In many cases, the need to adapt will be clear based on the nonverbal behaviors of audience members. However, speakers are often unsure of what the audience is communicating. For example, it may not be clear to the speaker based on nonverbal cues whether the audience could not hear what was said or if they disagreed with the message. If you are in doubt, ask **comprehension questions**. This is a special kind of question that seeks feedback from audience. For example, questions posed in conversational style by the speaker such as, "Does this make sense?" or "Would you like more information before we go on to the next topic?" following the description of a complex issue will help the speaker connect with the audience. If the audience members respond positively, the speaker continues with the presentation. If there does not appear to be an affirmative response to the question, the speaker needs to make a mid-course change and restate and clarify the information for the audience. Asking questions is a very useful method of gathering feedback during the presentation.

Effective speakers know that they must respond to what the audience is communicating, whether the message is agreement, disagreement, or disinterest. Consider the following question. How do you respond to people who ignore your messages? Probably not well. Few people respond positively to being ignored. By responding and adapting your message during the presentation, you communicate to the audience that you are aware of them and acknowledge their views.

Organizing and Outlining

In general, structured messages are more effective than unstructured messages. Without structure, if you achieve your goals it is by chance, not by design. Effective speakers do not rely on chance to achieve their goals. The structure and organization of your presentation will effect:

- How clearly the audience can follow and understand your speech.

- How the audience views your competence as a speaker.

- How confident you feel about your delivery.

In this section of the chapter, we will examine the key elements of presentation organization and structure.

MAIN POINTS

The main points are the key parts of your presentation and, taken together, make up your central idea. Without separate main points, the audience will not be able to follow your message. The main points reflect the key ideas that must be covered in the presentation in order to achieve your objective(s). In addition to grouping ideas, your goal is to develop main points that will stand out to the audience. In a sense, the main points function as road signs. When these signs are apparent to the audience, they have a clear road to follow. Without these road signs, it is hard for the audience to know where you (and they) are going.

ORGANIZATIONAL PATTERNS

For the purposes of this course, we will review five types of organization patterns that can be used to arrange the main points. You will decide which organizational pattern to use based on the specific purpose and central idea (main points).

CHAPTER 5

- **Chronological**. This pattern organizes your presentation in terms of time. It is used most often with informative presentations that involve a process or event. It is easier for an audience to follow a message that identifies steps or stages as they occur in time.

  Specific Purpose: To inform my audience about the five major steps associated with preparing a marketing campaign.

  Central Idea: The five major steps of preparing a marketing campaign include establishing marketing objectives, identifying the target market, identifying relevant attitudes, crafting the marketing message, and identifying appropriate message outlets.

- **Spatial**. This pattern is often used with informative presentations when discussing a topic that has shape or form, such as a building. The material in this pattern is organized in such a way that you discuss the topic from top to bottom or left to right.

  Specific Purpose: To inform my audience of the three major sections of the Empire State Building.

  Central Idea: The three major sections of the Empire State Building are the lowest section, the middle section, and the top section.

  Specific Purpose: To inform my audience about the three major regions of the state of Tennessee.

  Central Idea: The three major regions of the state of Tennessee are west, middle, and east Tennessee.

- **Causal**. This pattern indicates a cause-effect relationship exists between the two main points. One main point discusses the cause or causes of the event, and the other main point discusses the effect or effects of the cause. This pattern is appropriate for informative and persuasive presentations.

  Specific Purpose: To inform my audience of the three major causes of obesity.

  Central Idea: The three major causes of obesity are living a sedentary lifestyle, poor eating habits, and a genetic predisposition to weight gain.

- **Problem-Solution**. Most appropriate for persuasive presentations, the problem-solution pattern divides the message into two parts. The first part identifies the problem or problems that exist, while the second provides a solution or multiple solutions to the problem.

  Specific Purpose: To persuade my audience that a state law is needed to prohibit the use of cell phones while driving.

  Central Idea: The growing use of cell phones at the time of major vehicular accidents are creating a serious problem that can be solved by creating a law that prohibits the use of cell phones while driving.

- **Topical**. If the main points cannot be organized in one of the above patterns, divide the presentation into logical subtopics that become your main points. A topical pattern is used most often because of its suitability to merge several different issues in a single presentation. For example, an orientation presentation to new employees may cover several different topics, including a vision for the organization's future, job duties and responsibilities, and health and retirement benefits. This pattern of organizing is used in both informative and persuasive presentations.

  Specific Purpose: To inform my audience of the five major kinds of lottery tickets sold in Tennessee.

  Central Idea: The five major kinds of lottery tickets sold in Tennessee are Powerball, Cash Three, Tennessee Millionaire, Instant Payday, and Tennessee Treasures.

  Specific Purpose: To inform my audience about the five major accomplishments of Donald Trump.

  Central Idea: The five major accomplishments of Donald Trump's life are that he graduated from the Wharton School at the University of Pennsylvania in 1968, completed the Trump Tower, purchased the Taj Mahal Casino, built the Trump World Center, and starred on the NBC reality show, *The Apprentice*.

CHAPTER 5

Guidelines for Preparing Main Points

When preparing the main points, consider the following guidelines. First, limit the number of main points (possibly by combining main points). Second, main points should be distinct. That is, each main point should focus on a *single* idea. Third, when wording the main points, make certain that all of them are worded consistently for the purpose of clarity. It will be difficult for the audience to pick out your main points and follow your presentation if you do not word them in a similar fashion, as represented in the example below:

I. Genetic engineering is producing new plant hybrids that will vastly increase world agricultural production.

II. Genetic engineering is producing breakthroughs in medicine that will allow people to live healthier lives.

III. Genetic engineering is producing bacteria that will help clean up industrial pollutants.

Fourth, devote an approximately equal amount of time to each main point. It is unrealistic to think that you will devote exactly the same amount of time to each main point, but you should strive to balance the time between them as evenly as possible. If one main point is much longer than the others, it may mean the information in that main point needs to be separated into two main points. It could also mean that you need to condense the information to avoid repeating yourself within that point. It may also be that other main points do not include enough information to merit use as a main point. In this situation, you may need to combine similar main points or delete the information from the presentation.

Fifth, strategically order the main points. If you are using a chronological pattern of organization, the order of the main points is predetermined, since the steps or events will be presented in the order in which they occur. A presentation with a problem-solution pattern of organizing likely requires that the problem(s) be presented before the solution(s). It would be your decision when using a causal pattern whether or not you would discuss the cause(s) or effect(s) first. When using a topical or spatial organizational pattern, arrange the main points in a way that best lends itself to achieving your objectives.

SUPPORTING MATERIAL

Supporting material provides evidence to back up the ideas in your main points. All supporting materials should be directly relevant to the main points that they support. The supporting materials are needed by listeners in order to accept what is said by the speaker.

After you gather supporting materials (e.g., journal articles, newspaper stories, books, etc.), you are ready to organize your presentation by selecting the main points, writing the central idea, and grouping the supporting materials with the appropriate main point.

CONNECTIVES

Connectives are among the most important components to effective presentation organization. Connectives are words or phrases that link one thought to another and make clear the relationship between the two thoughts. They tie the presentation together by making it unified and coherent. Business communicators use several different kinds of connectives in presentations.

- **Transitions**. Transitions are sentences used between main points in the body of the presentation. Transitions tell the audience where you have been and where you are going. Transitions are the most important of all of the connectives, because they make clear to the audience the main points of the presentation.

  Example: "Now that we have covered the problem of outsourcing, let's discuss the solution to the problem."

- **Internal previews**. Internal previews are used to tell the listeners what will be covered next in the presentation. The most important internal preview in your presentation will be placed between the introduction and body. The central idea, discussed at the end of your introduction, is not considered an internal preview. An internal preview statement (like the one below) should come after the central idea and be located between the introduction and body of your message.

  Example: "First, I will talk about the problem of outsourcing."

- **Internal summaries**. This type of statement is the opposite of an internal preview, and is used only to recap for the audience what has been discussed. The most important internal summary will be in your conclusion before you recap the main points.

  Example: "In summary, I hope this presentation has given you a better understanding of the problem of outsourcing and how we can better solve this problem by revamping our manufacturing process."

- **Signposts**. These are words or brief statements that tell the audience where you are currently in the presentation. It is helpful to the audience if the speaker uses signposts throughout the presentation. They should be used between subpoints that support a main point.

  Example: An example of signposts includes the use of words such as "first," "second," "third," when discussing the order of information.

For connectives to be effective, the main points must be worded in a similar fashion throughout the presentation. Even minor word changes may confuse the audience.

CHAPTER 5

Preparing the Introduction and Conclusion

After completing the body of the presentation, you are ready to add the introduction and conclusion. Several features that we will discuss are appropriate for use in both the introduction and conclusion. To begin, the introduction to a presentation can serve several different functions. For the purposes of this course, we will focus on four objectives for the presentation introduction.

- **Gain the attention and interest of the audience**. When you begin the presentation, you must first include an attention-getter. Do not begin with your name and/or your topic. Several methods of gaining attention are commonly used by business communicators. Select a method that will allow you to relate to the audience. Please note: It is not appropriate to use two or more of these attention getting devices in a single introduction.

  - **State the importance of the topic**. You can convey the importance of the topic by giving a statistic that quantifies the importance of the topic or by giving a hypothetical example.

  - **Question the audience**. If questioning the audience, make it clear to the audience whether or not you want a response by saying something to the effect, "By a show of hands, how many of you plan to vote in the upcoming election?" Following this statement, wait for a response. If you do not require a response, just ask the audience members to think about their personal response. A word of caution about using questions: How will it impact your presentation if audience members respond in a way that you do not anticipate?

  - **Begin with a quote**. When quoting someone, do so in a way that is conversational so that the first item in your presentation is not being read. It is important to begin with a high level of eye contact in order to gain the attention of the audience.

  - **Tell a story**. Begin the presentation with a brief story. A word about the use of stories: If not worked out in advance, the delivery of the story will likely be longer and less well organized than you anticipated.

  - **Startle the audience**. This can be accomplished by including a shocking but appropriate statistic, example, or quotation.

  - **Arouse the curiosity of the audience**. You may choose to only tell part of a story to gain attention so your audience will continue to listen to find out what happened. You could also choose to give a statistic or example that does not give away the topic until later in your introduction. This is effective when you have novel information or an unfamiliar topic.

- **Reveal the purpose of the presentation.** Immediately after you gain the attention of the audience, state clearly the purpose of the presentation to avoid confusion. The only exception to this practice is in the event of intentionally deferring the purpose statement. This exception applies if you know that the audience will be actively hostile to your purpose. For example, if you represent an engineering consulting firm and are given the task of speaking to a group of concerned citizens about a proposed landfill next to their property, it would not be effective to state early in the introduction, "My purpose today is to persuade you to accept the location of the landfill next to your property." At that point the audience will no longer listen to the message, regardless of the evidence presented or the skill with which it is delivered. In this situation, the actual purpose would be deferred until your presentation prepares the audience to at least consider the goal.

- **Establish credibility as the speaker.** After gaining the attention of the audience and revealing the topic and purpose, tell the audience what connects you with the topic. Credibility in this case is a matter of being perceived by the audience as qualified to speak on a particular topic or being competent. Audience members make judgments of credibility based on two factors: perceptions of expertise and trust. The speaker must make a case in the eyes of the audience members that he or she is expert on this topic and is trustworthy.

- **Preview the body of the presentation (central idea).** The last component of the introduction is expected to be your central idea. As you recall, the central idea previews the body of the presentation by sharing with the audience your main points. This statement tells an audience what to listen for in the rest of the presentation, and, because it generally comes at the end of the introduction, the central idea provides a smooth lead-in to the body of the presentation.

Although it is clear that speakers seek to achieve certain objectives with the introduction, not every introduction is equally effective. In fact, speakers often find that developing an effective introduction is one of the most difficult parts of presentation preparation and delivery. When preparing your introduction, use the following criteria as a guide to developing the message.

- Did you address the four introduction objectives listed above?

- Did you define all unfamiliar/technical terms that will be used in the presentation?

- Is the introduction relatively brief?

- Is the introduction worked out in detail so it can be delivered effectively?

CONCLUSION FUNCTIONS

Consistent with the introduction, the conclusion also serves a number of important functions. These functions include the following:

- **Signals the end of the presentation**. Although this may seem obvious, it is important to let the audience know when you have reached the presentation conclusion. Abrupt endings leave listeners surprised and unfulfilled. If you do not begin your conclusion with a statement such as "in summary" or some other connective, the audience may not know where you are in the presentation.

- **Summarize the main points of the presentation**. You should reinforce the audience's understanding of and commitment to the central idea by recapping your main points for the audience. For example, you may want to word your recap something like "I hope that you have a better understanding…"

- **End with a dramatic, final statement**. As your attention-gaining device is the first element of an introduction, your final statement is the last element of your presentation and what the audience is most likely to remember. Ask yourself what you want the audience to take away from the presentation. The "take-away" may be tied to a famous quote or to a current event that is impacting the audience's company/industry. You may choose to refer back to an item mentioned in the introduction and offer a concluding view of that item. Whatever you select, make the concluding statements memorable.

GUIDELINES FOR PREPARING AN EFFECTIVE CONCLUSION

As with introductions, not all conclusions are equally effective. Speakers often succeed or fail to develop effective conclusions based on the following criteria:

- Conclude on a strong note; leave the audience with something memorable.

- Be relatively brief.

- Avoid introducing ideas/information in the conclusion that were not covered in the body of the presentation.

Outlining the Presentation

Outlining the presentation is important in the organization of the material. Two different kinds of outlines exist. The **preparation outline** is the full representation of the entire presentation. In effect, if someone had your preparation outline in front of him or her, that person would be able to follow along throughout the presentation. In many business and professional presentations, the speaker may provide audience members a preparation outline as part of the event.

A second type of outline, the **speaking outline**, often serves as the notes that the speaker uses during the presentation. Effective speakers make use of both types of outlines. Following completion of the preparation outline, you should transfer the most important parts of it to a speaking outline format before you begin to practice. Some issues to consider when developing a speaking outline from the preparation outline are:

- **Use the same outline form for both outlines**. This will help you find content easily during the presentation.

- **Keep the outline brief**. The speaking outline is much more concise than a preparation outline. Thus, you will not be tempted to read your presentation instead of delivering it extemporaneously. Complete sentences are not required for the speaking outline; phrases and words are sufficient unless you are quoting someone.

- **Make it legible**. Although this may appear obvious, it is surprising how many people create notes that they later cannot follow. One way to be certain that the information on your speaking outline is legible is to type your notes with a larger-than-usual type size.

- **Use only one side of the paper/note cards**. Keeping track of notes is made more difficult if you record information on the front and back of the note cards or paper. In addition, number the note cards so that they can be tracked and ordered more easily.

- **Include delivery cues**. Include cues or reminders to say or do something at specific times during the presentation. The rule of thumb when preparing a speaking outline is to include what you need to deliver the presentation effectively.

Preparing Visual Aids

When delivering presentations in the business world, it is common to use the visual aids that are supplied by the company. In fact, many organizations have policies about what can be used and/or how information must be displayed, such as company logos. For example, Winpak, a company that manufactures and distributes packaging materials and packaging machines for health care applications, has clear policies on what can be said and how visuals are to be used, as illustrated by the following statement:

> Communication of prepared presentations to, and discussions with, limited groups will be conducted on a basis consistent with each other. The Company will retain records of meetings and communications with financial analysts and investors, if situations arise that are, in the view of the Spokespersons, unusual or could require reference at a later date.
>
> Source: http://www.winpak.com/en/company/1-1-0-2.htm

Thus, when preparing visual aids over the course of your career, make certain that you conform to whatever expectations the organization has for materials used as visual aids. Not surprisingly, most all companies have a keen interest in how the business is visually portrayed.

As you can see, visual aids are an important but controversial component to business presentations. The decision to use visual aids should be driven by whether or not the visual aids help the speaker achieve his/her goals. Thus, if you choose to use visual aids for a presentation in this course, be certain that they are necessary to achieve your objectives. Visual aids must not be used as a substitute for the speaker.

Visual aids are used to enhance presentations. The visual aids do not determine the goal of the presentation or its main points. In this chapter, we will discuss the advantages of using visual aids, the types of visual aids, how to prepare visual aids, and how to present visual aids effectively. If you are *not* using a visual aid for one of the reasons below you should reconsider its use. When in doubt about the use of a visual aid, speak with your instructor.

There are several major advantages of using visual aids. However, visual aids are not necessary or even appropriate for all presentations. When deciding whether to use visual aids, ask yourself if their use will advance your objectives in the following ways:

- **Adding clarity**. Since one of the major goals of any type of presentation is to be clear, this is the primary advantage of using visual aids. There may be portions of your presentation that are difficult to explain or describe. Visual aids are an effective tool for clarifying complex ideas that do not lend themselves to simple, clear language. If your visual aids are not clear, they will be worse than useless. They will confuse the audience.

- **Adding interest**. Visual aids are often used to attract attention as well as spark curiosity about your topic. Look over your outline and consider whether some areas of the presentation are not as interesting as others. In such cases, you may want to add a visual aid to strengthen the supporting material used in that portion of the presentation.

- **Aiding in retention**. You may also want to pick out material in the presentation that you want to stand out and make memorable. Keep in mind that visual aids that make use of images tend to be more memorable than visuals that rely exclusively on text.

TYPES OF VISUAL AIDS

There are several types of visual aids that are used in business presentations. Your selection and use of visual aids will be determined by the specific purpose and the nature of the supporting material. Although numerous items may serve as visual aids, for the purpose of this course we will focus on objects, models, photographs, drawings, graphs, audio/video recordings, and handouts.

Objects

One way to clarify ideas and provide a dramatic impact is to bring an object of what you are discussing. Objects may include equipment, devices, or even other people. For example, if you are delivering an informative presentation in support of a wellness fair, you may want to bring equipment used in the wellness fair (blood pressure devices, etc.) to show your audience. Keep in mind that the object that is used must be large enough to be visible to all members of the audience. Moreover, objects such as live animals, firearms, or illegal substances are not permitted and are against university policy.

Models

A model is a simplified version of the real thing. As a visual aid in a presentation, models tend to be either small-scale replicas of a large object, a large-scale replica of a small object, or a life-size representation of the real object. For example, if you were delivering a presentation about the design of a building, you may want to bring a model of the building. As noted previously, the model must be large enough for all members of the audience to see easily.

Photographs

Photographs are useful for displaying information about places, people, or objects. Photographs should be incorporated into presentation software (e.g., PowerPoint) for display, since photos typically are too small to be viewed by audience members.

Drawings

Sketches, diagrams, and illustrations are types of drawings, and when prepared properly can be a very effective way to support your material. A presentation about plans for a future building may include an architectural drawing of floor plans. If explaining dyslexia to an audience, the speaker may prepare a drawing of what a sentence looks like to those with dyslexia.

Graphs and Charts

This catch phrase refers to a wide variety of ways to display numeric data. A number of different graphs and charts are commonly used to clarify statistics, including line graphs, bar graphs, and pie graphs. These types of visual aids allow audience members to more readily grasp information that may be difficult or impossible to follow in the verbal portion of the presentation. Perhaps most important, graphs and charts can make clear relationships between numbers. As with photographs, graphs and charts should be incorporated into presentation software.

Audio-Video Recordings

Advances in communication technology allow presenters to draw from a wide range of audio-visual recordings for use as visual aids (e.g., a company-prepared video, commercial, documentary, etc.) to illustrate a point. This type of visual aid offers advantages in terms of the power to bring multiple visuals involving both sound and images to the presentation. However, choosing to use electronically recorded information will complicate the preparation process for many reasons. First, the timing associated with the use of the visual needs to be calculated to make sure you have enough time in your presentation for the material. Second, other visual aids allow you to talk while displaying them, but that may not be possible with this type of visual unless the audio portion is muted. Third, you will in effect lose a portion of the time available to you as the speaker when using this type of visual aid. Fourth, the video must be cued and ready to play the scene you wish to show. Fifth, because the equipment may fail, you must be prepared to adapt and deliver a presentation without visual aids.

CHAPTER 5

The major multimedia presentation tool available to you that can handle both audio and visual components is Microsoft PowerPoint. When you use PowerPoint as a multimedia presentation, you are combining two or more slides to show during some or all of the presentation. To aid you in developing presentations, all of the computer labs on the UT campus are outfitted with PowerPoint software. Moreover, the Media Center in Hodges Library has equipment and staff to assist you in creating presentations. For an online PowerPoint tutorial, visit the School of Communication Studies Web page at: http://www.cci.utk.edu/commstudies/oral.

Handouts

Finally, depending on your information, there may be something that you will want the audience to keep and/or refer to during the presentation. In this case, it would be appropriate to make use of a handout. For example, if you were delivering an informative presentation to a group of new employees, it would be appropriate to use handouts that support your presentation while offering audience members the opportunity to keep important information.

GUIDELINES FOR PREPARING VISUAL AIDS

The following guidelines will aid you when preparing visual aids for this course, as well as throughout your career:

Preparing All Types of Visual Aids

- **Prepare visual aids after preparing your presentation**. Do not prepare visual aids or even decide upon them until your entire presentation is complete. Upon completion, review the outline and decide what is needed to advance your presentation objectives.

- **Prepare visual aids before you practice**. You will derive limited benefit from practicing the presentation if your visual aids are not available.

- **Keep visual aids simple**. Less is more! If your goal is to be clear to the audience, keep it simple. Elaborate visual aids are distracting and confusing to the audience.

- **Make sure visual aids are large enough to be seen**. The visual aid will not clarify, increase interest, or help the audience retain your message if it is too small. Remember—everyone in the audience must be able to see the visual aid. No exceptions!

Preparing PowerPoint Slides
(visit: http://www.cci.utk.edu/commstudies/oral)
- **Do not use full sentences**. The most important guideline to preparing PowerPoint slides and the biggest mistake that students make is to use too much text on slides. Use text sparingly! The text must not replace the information the audience receives verbally; the text should clarify and make your message memorable.

- **Use color effectively**. Use a limited number of contrasting colors on slides. Too many colors will become a distraction to the audience. When selecting the colors for the background and the text, make sure to use a light color with one and a dark color with the other. For example, selecting a black background in conjunction with purple text will make it difficult or impossible for the audience to see the text. In addition, make certain that the colors associated with graphs are clearly differentiated.

- **Choose font types wisely**. Avoid using decorative and distractive fonts that are difficult to read.

- **Make type sizes large enough**. You must use a type size that is large enough to be seen by the entire audience. Usually, the "default" type size that appears on a new slide is appropriate. A large enough type size to be seen clearly is 44-point for titles and 32-point for text. In fact, you should make the type larger if room is available on the slide.

- **All slides should be consistent**. The background, font, and colors that you choose for slides should be consistent throughout the presentation. Consistency makes it easier for the audience to read and recognize the information on the slides.

- **Use space effectively**. Avoid large blank spaces on a slide. Try to use the entire slide or combine information onto one slide. However, do not put too much material on a single slide, because you do not want the audience to be overwhelmed by the slide's complexity.

- **Avoid sound**. Make sure that the animation sounds are turned off. Any unnecessary sound will only distract you and your audience.

- **Avoid unnecessary animation**. In PowerPoint, custom animation allows you to have your text and graphics appear through decorative animation such as scrolling or flying into the slide. You need to make sure when you custom-animate your slides for timing you click on "appear," so it only appears when you advance your slides.

- **Avoid clip art**. Clip art is unnecessary. Pictures of anything needed for display are readily available from many sources.

- **Use blank slides when necessary**. Make use of blank slides in the portions of the presentation in which no visual aid is needed. The entire presentation will not require constant use of PowerPoint. Rather, PowerPoint slides will only be needed for selected portions of the presentation.

- **Avoid a title slide**. It is inappropriate to include your title and name on the first slide. The first slide should be blank or include whatever you are using as the attention-gaining device.

CHAPTER 5

- **Avoid timing your slides**. Advance the slides manually so that you can adjust the pace of the presentation based on audience response. Do not elect to advance the slides on a schedule (e.g., every 30 seconds).

- **Write presentation cues on speaking outline**. To remind yourself when to advance slides, include cues on your speaking outline or note cards.

GUIDELINES FOR PRESENTING VISUAL AIDS

The use of visual aids will have considerable impact on the outcome of the presentation (and the presentation grade!). Make use of the following guidelines when presenting the visual aids:

- **Avoid using the chalkboard/whiteboard**. Using the chalkboard or whiteboard is not appropriate for several reasons. It forces you to turn your back to the audience and lose eye contact, it takes more time to present the information, it can be messy, and it reduces your credibility by suggesting to the audience that you have not taken the time and effort to adequately prepare for the presentation.

- **The visual must be visible to all members of the audience**.

- **Avoid passing out visual aids during the presentation**. Offer handouts at the conclusion of the presentation. If you must use a handout during the presentation, manage how audience members use it by directing them to specific information or images.

- **Display visuals only when discussing them**. Visual aids should be visible only when the speaker is referring to them. When not in use, the visual should be turned off or masked in some way so as not to distract the audience.

- **Explain the visual clearly**. Explain to the audience what they are seeing. Do not assume that the meaning of the visual is obvious to audience members.

- **Talk to the audience, not the visual aid**. Maintain eye contact with the audience even when showing and explaining a visual aid.

Practicing the Presentation

Practice does not always make perfect, but it does make permanent. Thus, take practice seriously and mimic as closely as possible the practice conditions with the actual presentation setting. The more frequently you rehearse, the more prepared you will feel. This feeling of being prepared will help to reduce nervousness and will further your credibility with the audience. The following steps will help to make your practice time productive:

- Read the speaking outline aloud several times, adding any needed material.

- Talk through all examples and stories.

- Recite in full all quotations and statistics.

- Use visual aids as you practice so you become comfortable presenting them.

- Practice the entire presentation, even if you make mistakes. Don't stop!

- After the first few trials, begin to keep time in order to determine what, if anything, must be added or deleted to stay within the allotted time.

- Concentrate on gaining control of the ideas and engaging in a conversation with the audience, instead of trying to learn the presentation word for word.

- Practice the presentation in front of friends, roommates, family, etc., for honest feedback on eye contact and distracting mannerisms. You will find it helpful to get their opinions about how well you explained your ideas.

Key Terms

Audience analysis

Adapting to feedback

Patterns of organizing

Introductions and conclusions

Presentation outline and speaking outline

Visual aids

CHAPTER 5

CHAPTER 6

BUSINESS PRESENTATIONS: DELIVERY

Overview

When you think of any presentation, you will think of it as including two components—content and delivery. Presentation delivery involves how you present the message and includes how you sound, how you look, and what you do nonverbally during a presentation. Because delivery is one of the most important parts of the presentation process, it is helpful to know what counts as good or effective presentation delivery. Simply put, effective does not call attention to itself. Thus, the receivers are able to focus on the message rather than any other delivery-related factor. Effective delivery is characterized by two qualities: naturalness and conversational quality.

Receivers tend to be distracted by a speaker's voice or body movement. Therefore, a natural speaking style that does not call attention to itself is more effective. It conveys the speaker's ideas clearly, in an interesting fashion and without distracting the audience. If you project your voice poorly, make little or no eye contact, shuffle your feet, or speak in a monotone voice, you will not reach the audience. Thus, good presentation delivery appears both natural and conversational, even though it has been rehearsed. In this chapter we will explore the factors that contribute to effective delivery. Specifically, we will examine different methods of delivery, delivery styles, use of voice, and nonverbal communication.

Methods of Delivery

The first method of delivery is **impromptu**. You may be delivering several short presentations using this method. An impromptu method of delivery involves little or no preparation. The assignments that require the use of an impromptu method will help you think more quickly and effectively "off the cuff." This is not, however, the method that you will use to deliver major assignments in this course, such as the informative, persuasive, or special occasion presentations.

In Chapter Six, you will learn about:

- Four Methods of Presentation Delivery

- The Important Components of the Speaker's Voice: Volume, Rate, Pauses, Vocal Variety, and Articulation

- The Important Components of Nonverbal Communication: Eye Contact, Body Action, and Gestures

The second method of delivery involves **reading from a manuscript**. Reading from a manuscript is acceptable in special circumstances, such as a presentation that is delivered by a diplomat to the United Nations. In this special kind of setting, it is essential that every word is stated exactly as prepared. This method of delivery *will not* be acceptable for use in this class. If you look back to the syllabus, you will see that any presentation that is read will receive no grade above a "C." When you read from a manuscript, you are unable to adapt your message to the audience. Effective presentations are characterized by speaker flexibility and adaptiveness.

The third method of delivery involves **reciting the presentation from memory**. As with reading, reciting from memory is not an effective method of delivery. Since the presentation is memorized, the speaker is unable to adapt his/her message to the audience. Moreover, this method is not natural and tends to distract the audience. That is, this method makes your voice sound robotic and it lacks vocal variety.

The major goal of the unit on delivery is to develop your skills as an **extemporaneous** speaker, the fourth method of delivery. An extemporaneous presentation is carefully prepared and rehearsed, and is presented from a brief set of notes. Even though it is fully prepared ahead of time, the exact words are not chosen until the moment of delivery. This is why it is different from a presentation recited from memory. This will seem difficult at first because you will know the material well as a result of both preparation and practice. The key is to not memorize words or even phrases, but to learn or "grasp" the ideas of your presentation. This means that each time you practice, you will discuss the same ideas but will use different words. The key to being extemporaneous is to be conversational with your audience.

Conversational Quality

Being extemporaneous also means that you will make use of a natural, conversational style of delivery. Many people approach business presentations with the idea that it requires a totally different way of communicating. Effective speakers realize that the conversational qualities that lead to success in interpersonal or group situations apply to business communication situations. You will talk and use nonverbal communication in much the same way you would in an ordinary conversation. Approaching your presentation with a bit less formality will help you develop an extemporaneous, conversational style of delivery. As we discussed earlier, seek to communicate, not perform.

USE OF VOICE

Your voice is very important to your credibility. For the audience to receive your message clearly and without distraction, your voice must be used in a comprehensible, non-distracting manner. The following information reviews the eight voice factors that will influence your performance.

Volume

Simply put, speak loudly enough for all in the room to hear. If you do not project your voice, you will not convey your message to the audience. Most likely, you will need to project your voice more fully than you anticipate in order to be heard by all audience members. In many rooms, sound escapes or is absorbed by walls, desks, etc. In addition, there may be outside noise that competes with your voice. Practice the presentation with a greater volume than you expect to use during the presentation. Do not force your listeners to strain in order to hear you. You cannot command attention by speaking softly.

Rate

Rate involves the speed with which you speak. Your objective is to speak at a rate that maintains audience interest and that does not distract the audience from the message. Many students need to slow down their speaking rate as a result of nervousness. When people get nervous, they tend to speak faster than is normal in day-to-day conversations. When you speak too fast, the audience lacks the time to take in your ideas and reflect on them. A faster-than-normal delivery rate can also present problems with articulation. Speaking at a fast rate tends to run together all the vowel sounds and, as a result, you will be very difficult to understand. On the other hand, if you are one of the few who speak too slowly, speak a bit faster so that you maintain the attention of the audience.

Pitch

Pitch involves the highness or lowness of voice. Overall, your objective is to speak in even tones. Have you ever listened to someone's voice that was so high pitched that it sounded like fingernails down a chalkboard? Similarly, have you listened to a voice so "muddy" and low that it distracts from the message? If the tone of your voice is too high or low, practice speaking in even tones so that your pitch doesn't distract your audience.

Vocal Variety

Changes in rate, pitch, and volume that give the voice expressiveness are considered vocal variety. Think about this as the opposite of being monotone and boring. If you read a story to a group of children, you would likely use a great deal of inflection in your voice to make it interesting to them. You need to do the same during presentations to keep the audience interested. Most of us could stand to use more variety in our voices, since it is a very effective tool to maintain audience interest in the message. However, students often report that they feel uncomfortable with vocal variety because it seems theatrical or possibly even fake. If you practice the use of vocal variety in conversations it will become natural and, as a result, people will perceive you as more interesting. Consider how much you enjoy listening to actors who have a very expressive voice (and how much you are willing to pay to listen!) at movie theaters.

Pauses

Momentary breaks in vocal delivery are pauses. Silent pauses between ideas and/or some sentences are very effective. For example, we understand that a speaker must pause before the punch line of a joke. The pause alerts the listeners to the punch line. Without a pause, the impact of the message is diminished. In addition to acting as a signal to the audience, pauses help the speaker manage his or her rate of delivery. Simply put, it forces the speaker to slow down. However, not all pauses are effective.

Vocalized Pauses

Vocalized pauses are filler words that are inappropriate to use in a presentation such as "uh," "um," "like," or "you know." Vocalized pauses are very distracting for listeners and the credibility of a speaker is diminished as their use increases. One useful technique to become aware of your own use of vocalized pauses is to record yourself while practicing a presentation. As you listen to the recording and continue to practice, seek to replace these vocalized pauses with silent pauses.

Pronunciation

The accepted standard of sound and rhythm is pronunciation. Make sure to familiarize yourself with all unfamiliar words, especially the **proper names** that you cite. If you anticipate difficultly pronouncing a word, find synonyms for it before you begin to practice. Your credibility as a speaker is diminished when you mispronounce words or names.

Articulation

The physical production of sounds is considered articulation. More specifically, our concern here is with your skill with stating the words in the presentation clearly and distinctly. Simply put, effective speakers sound out words correctly.

Dialect

The variations of accent, grammar, or vocabulary are considered dialect. As a business communicator, you will encounter situations in which audience members are not from your hometown, your region, or your country. Individuals in your audience may embrace different cultures and speak with different accents. This course is not designed to change your accent. However, you should record yourself to determine if you possess a strong accent. If you do, make sure to practice and master all of the voice factors discussed in this section. Mastering these factors will help you to compensate for a strong accent. Also, make sure to use grammar correctly and choose your vocabulary carefully. Have others listen to you and offer suggestions on more appropriate forms of grammar/vocabulary. For many, a deficiency in one aspect of how a voice is used carries over to other aspects. As you continue through the semester, you will begin to understand which aspects of your voice are considered strengths, as well as the aspects of your voice that need to be strengthened.

Nonverbal Communication

Your delivery is not only impacted by your voice, but also by your nonverbal cues. Audience members will listen to you and watch you. In general, a speaker's nonverbal communication tends to be viewed as more accurate by audience members than the verbal portion of the message. Simply put, we tend to believe what we see rather than what we hear. Thus, being consciously aware of and skillfully managing your nonverbal messages will more likely lead you to achieve your goals for the presentation. Consistent with your use of voice, make sure that your nonverbal communication does not distract the audience from focusing on the verbal portion of the message. For the purposes of this course, we will focus our attention on four nonverbal behaviors that accompany business presentations. These four focus areas include:

Eye Contact

During a presentation, you will be expected to maintain eye contact with the audience as you speak. Next to an extemporaneous and conversational speaking style, eye contact is the most important factor in the delivery of your message. Adequate preparation for a presentation allows you to use the majority of the time looking at your audience rather than your notes. This is why eye contact is essential to the use of an extemporaneous, conversational speaking style. For example, if you are reading your presentation it will not be possible to maintain eye contact with the audience. Do not look at the back wall over the heads of the listeners—look them in the eye. You must maintain approximately equal eye contact with all members of the audience—not just one side of the room. Practice scanning the room back and forth. Your eyes should convey confidence, sincerity, and conviction. Effective speakers maintain eye contact with the audience throughout the presentation. Whatever the length of the presentation, eye contact with the audience should be maintained for approximately 70–80 percent of the presentation.

Body Movement

Speakers vary in how they use their bodies during the course of a presentation. For some, their body movement distracts the audience. The kind of distracting mannerisms speakers should avoid include swaying back and forth, tapping, and pacing. To keep from distracting your audience, practice good posture by standing with your feet shoulder-width apart while maintaining approximately equal weight on each foot. This posture will keep you from swaying or bouncing while giving you confidence and credibility.

Gestures

Gestures involve the motions of both your hands and arms. Effective gestures are natural and do not call attention to themselves. There is nothing wrong with talking with your hands, as long as these gestures are not forced or robotic, and are not excessive. Ineffective gestures are robotic, overdone, and unnatural. Ineffective gesturing includes clenching the podium, putting your hands in your pockets, waving your hands excessively, or clasping your hands behind your back. Many students find that they don't know what to do with their hands while speaking. If you are using the podium, hold your notes up and rest your wrists on the podium, or place your notes on the podium and rest your hands lightly on the edges of the podium. Be cautious about gesturing with note cards in your hand, since they may inadvertently fly away. Keep in mind the following: If you use your hands in the presentation the way you naturally use them in conversation, you will likely perform well.

Personal Appearance

The rule of thumb is to dress professionally but comfortably. As discussed earlier, you will not be viewed as a credible speaker unless you look the part. If you look professional you will perform in a more professional manner. Do wear business casual clothing and comfortable shoes. Do not wear T-shirts, hats, shirts with illustrations or messages on them, jeans or other pants with holes, shorts, athletic apparel, or revealing clothing. If you think it may be inappropriate, do not wear it. Ask your instructor for specific guidelines concerning your presentation attire.

Personal appearance also includes grooming. On the days that you are scheduled to deliver a presentation, make sure to appear well groomed. These guidelines are in place to boost your credibility. Just as with other nonverbal cues, your personal appearance could distract the audience from your message.

Remember that others will react to your nonverbal cues from the time you leave your seat until the time you return to it. This is true for this course as well as for your future workplace experiences. Therefore, your nonverbal behavior should be composed both before and after your presentation. The more you practice your delivery, the better and more comfortable you will be. Practice does not always make perfect, but it does make permanent.

Addressing Audience Questions

Brief question-and-answer sessions often follow informative and persuasive presentations. After you enter the business world, it will be your responsibility to determine if the situation calls for a question-and-answer session *or* be prepared to conform to this practice if it is expected by members of that organization. If you engage in such a session, ask members of the audience if there are questions *after* you have concluded the presentation. During the preparation process, it is possible to begin to formulate answers to possible questions from the audience. When preparing for the question-and-answer session, consider the following guidelines.

- Take it as seriously as the presentation itself. Your presentation begins from the time you leave your seat and does not end until you return to it.

- Use the same conversational delivery style that you have for the presentation itself. Do not become someone else after your presentation is concluded.

- Approach questions with a positive attitude. Do not assume that the aim is to embarrass you or trip you up.

- Listen carefully to the question that is being asked so that you do not mistakenly answer a question that was not asked.

- Answer only the question that has been asked. Do not offer further explanations or information items that you may have left out during your presentation.

- Repeat the question for the entire audience if you believe that the question was not heard by everyone. This will help every listener feel that he/she is involved in the session.

- Direct your answers to the entire audience and not just the person who asked the question. This practice will help you to involve the entire audience in the Q&A session and make them feel like active participants.

- Be honest and straightforward. If you do not know the answer to a question, acknowledge it. Your audience is certain to discover your dishonesty and lose trust in you as a credible speaker. If you do not know an answer, simply respond by indicating, "I did not run across that in my research, but I will try to find out and get back to you."

Key Terms

Presentation delivery

Methods of delivery

    Impromptu

    Reading from a manuscript

    Memorized

    Extemporaneous

Naturalness

Conversational quality

Use of voice

Nonverbal communication

Question-and-answer sessions

CHAPTER 7

INFORMATIVE, PERSUASIVE, GROUP, AND SPECIAL OCCASION PRESENTATIONS

Overview

Presentations take place on an almost daily basis in organizations. It is a common method of reporting on the status of a project, briefing audience members about policies and procedures, marketing products or services, and making employees aware of changes taking place in the company. In previous chapters, you explored presentation preparation and delivery factors that are common across most all types of presentations. In the following section, you will learn how to tailor presentations to the general goals identified earlier: To inform, to persuade, and to entertain.

Informative Presentations

Informative presentations provide a context in which many different members of a company can hear the same information from a single source. This type of presentation allows for relatively speedy dissemination of information within an organization. While the principles discussed earlier apply to this kind of presentation, the following guidelines will help you to tailor your preparation and delivery to this type of objective.

In Chapter Seven, you will learn about:

- Guidelines for Informative Presentations

- Definitions of Persuasion

- The Target Audience

- Three Types of Persuasive Presentations

- Five Steps of Monroe's Motivated Sequence

- Two Most Important Factors that Affect Source Credibility

- Four Factors that Affect Message Content

- Four Ways to Use Evidence in a Persuasive Presentation

- Reasoning

- Fallacies

- Group Presentation Guidelines

- Types of Special Occasion Presentations

INFORMATIVE PRESENTATION GUIDELINES

- **Do not overestimate what the audience knows**. It is easy to assume that because you know a lot about topic, your audience does too. Generally, the person delivering the informative presentation is well versed in the topic, but others may not be as clear on one or more aspects of what is to be discussed. Remember that they are hearing much of this information for the first time. (Otherwise, why hold the presentation?)

- **Be clear, direct, and specific**. Effective informative presentations tend not to be generic in nature. That is, this type of presentation calls for a clearly understood objective and supporting information that is specific and relevant.

- **Do not use jargon**. Avoid using technical terms that your audience will not understand. As you are searching for information, consider paraphrasing complicated information in order for your audience to comprehend the content faster and easier. It is often easy to become prisoner to the terms and jargon used in an organization, but their use may present problems in this type of presentation. Consider your experience here at UT. What is a DARS report? If you were delivering an informative presentation to a group of prospective students, how would you explain a DARS report? If clarity is the goal, use the simplest terms possible so the audience will not be confused. (A hint: The DARS report refers to Degree Audit Reporting System and is something your advisor reviews during an advising session.)

- **Avoid abstractions**. The first goal of informative speaking is to be clear. Therefore, make sure you explain the information thoroughly. The best way to avoid being abstract is to use concrete language.

- **Personalize your ideas**. Present your thoughts in human terms that relate to the experiences of the audience. Do not be afraid to use your own experiences to bring the material to life. You want the audience to identify with you and your presentation, so learn what experiences are common to you and the audience members.

- **Avoid persuasion**. Avoid the temptation of introducing a persuasive note into this presentation. Focus on the goal of informing. Your success will be determined by whether audience members walked away more fully informed about the topic.

- **Be prepared to answer questions**. Informative presentations in the workplace are often accompanied by question-and-answer sessions. As noted previously, your goal is not to persuade but to inform, and that objective applies to the question-and-answer session as well as to the presentation.

The Case of the RIDB

Not familiar with RIDB? It stands for the Readiness Integrated Database. The people working on this database are employees of the U.S. Department of Defense. The goal of this group is to determine the combat readiness level of U.S. Army units worldwide. It is common for members of this group to deliver as well as receive informative presentations about the status of various projects. Moreover, the people at these presentations represent vendors (suppliers) as well as Army and Defense Department Personnel. In one such situation, a member of the RIDB unit was delivering an informative presentation to several vendors about the technical requirements for a laptop computer that is a required piece of equipment for most Army units. The goal of the presentation was to update those involved on the status of a project to update the computers. Each audience member represented company (vendor) supplying equipment and/or parts for the project.

The person delivering the presentation began by stating, "DARCOM has tasked RIDB to develop AWAC-compatible technology for this project by FY-2010. The OR office at MRSA is acting in an advisory capacity to this project…" Mike Lynn, a new employee with Boeing Aviation, is one of the vendors in the audience listening to this presentation and doesn't quite know how to respond. He doesn't have a clue as to what all this jargon is about or what these acronyms mean.

What should he do?

Persuasive Presentations

People are exposed to persuasive messages on a daily basis. You may try to talk your friend into going out, ask your parents for money, or watch commercials that seek to sell you a product or service. In some instances, the goal of the sender is achieved. In most cases, receivers reject the persuasive appeal. For people in a wide variety of careers, such as government and politics, public relations, advertising, sales, management, and coaching, persuasive speaking skills are a necessary ingredient for success. Thus, it is not surprising that many people are interested in knowing more about persuasion and how it works. In this chapter we will define persuasion, discuss how persuasion is believed to work, and describe how to develop a persuasive presentation.

PERSUASION DEFINED

Like communication, persuasion has been a difficult concept to define. Most agree that persuasion should be defined as involving some measure of change in attitudes and/or behaviors. In addition, most all definitions agree that persuasion is a **receiver-oriented** area of study. That is, our principle concern is with how receivers process and are influenced by persuasive messages. However, there is less agreement about other aspects of a definition of persuasion. Consider the following questions:

- Is the message considered "persuasion" if the speaker *does not* achieve his or her objectives? The answer to this question has very practical implications. If you believe that persuasion should be defined so that the speaker must achieve his/her goals in changing attitudes or behaviors, how do you view an unsuccessful attempt at changing the attitudes or behaviors of the audience? Is it success or is it the attempt to persuade that should fall within our definition? What should your grade be on the persuasive speaking assignment if you deliver a good presentation but fail to influence the attitudes or behaviors of audience members? If you are in sales, is persuasion the skillful delivery of a message, or actually closing the sale?

- Is the message "persuasion" when the sender does not act in good faith and make clear his or her intentions? If a speaker influences you to change behaviors "for your own good" but the speaker's true intention is to benefit him or herself, has persuasion taken place? Or, was this manipulation?

At its core, persuasion involves the changing or reinforcing of attitudes and/or behaviors. We will adopt the working definition used by O'Keefe for **persuasion** as the intentional influencing of a receiver's attitudes and/or behaviors through communication.

HOW PERSUASION WORKS

Persuasion takes place when messages influence the attitudes and/or behaviors of receivers. However, no one has actually "seen" how persuasion works. That is, no one has actually viewed what a message does when it collides with an attitude that exists in your mind. Researchers have developed a wide range of theories that attempt to explain what happens when persuasion occurs. One way to understand this body of research on persuasion and how it works is to examine the key factors that make a difference when persuasion is taking place. Effective presenters understand that these factors will impact their ability to achieve persuasive objectives. These factors will be particularly important to consider when you are seeking to influence the **target audience**. The target audience consists of the group of people that you are most interested in influencing during the presentation. For example, students often target teachers during in-class presentations, since teachers assign grades and classmates do not. For students, teachers tend to be the target audience. However, because audience relevance is so much more important in a persuasive presentation, it is imperative that you, as a speaker, determine your target audience. Regardless of skill level, it is difficult for a speaker to persuade all audience members. Because the act of persuasion deals with people's attitudes or behaviors, it is unrealistic to think that your presentation will influence every audience member the way you desire. Determining your target audience will help you establish a realistic goal for yourself. Consider diagramming your target audience as explained in the following figure:

TARGET AUDIENCE ATTITUDE CHANGE MODEL

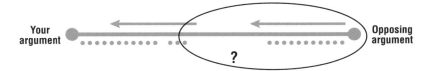

The line represents your purpose as a speaker. The dots represent audience members and where they stand in their attitudes or behaviors regarding your topic. The question mark (identified with the symbol ?) inside the circle represents people who are unsure, do not know, do not care, or do not have an opinion. The members of the audience plotted to the left of the line already agree with you or are currently doing what you seek. Thus, you are only reinforcing their attitudes or behaviors through your presentation. Therefore, your target audience includes all audience members who disagree with you *and* who are in the middle ground, located within the circle above. As noted, it would be unrealistic to assume that all audience members will be plotted on the left side by the end of your presentation. If persuasion deals with change, then your goal should be to bring each closer to your side represented by the arrows. You want each member of your target audience to be *closer* to your side by the end of your presentation. This means that the listeners on the right should be closer toward the middle and thinking about changing their attitudes or behaviors. This should help you better understand your purpose so you do not become overwhelmed by all you must accomplish.

TYPES OF PERSUASIVE PRESENTATIONS/ORGANIZATIONAL PATTERNS

There are several different types of persuasive presentations. For many people, persuasive presentations are put into categories on the basis of the type of question the speaker is seeking to answer. The use of questions underscores the role of controversy in persuasion: There is often more than one answer to a question. The three different types of persuasive presentations are designed to address:

Questions of Fact

Persuasive presentations that address questions of fact focus on the truth of a claim or assertion. Simply put, the persuasive message attempts to answer "what is." This may seem to contradict our common-sense understanding that facts are beyond dispute. In this type of persuasive presentation, the speaker is asserting that the label (fact) we have assigned to some kind of information is not valid, or that previously unlabeled information should be assigned the label "fact." Facts about the physical world are easier to establish than facts about our social world. A **topical** pattern of organization is best suited to persuasive presentations designed to address questions of fact. The main points in the body should include your arguments as to the reasons the "fact" is true or false.

Specific Purpose: To persuade National Science Foundation members in attendance that life currently exists on Mars.

Central Idea: The two major reasons life currently exists on Mars are the discovery of pockets of water and the finding of methane signatures and similar signs of possible biological activity remarkably similar to those recently discovered in caves here on Earth.

Specific Purpose: To persuade my audience that genetically engineered crops pose serious dangers to the environment and to human health.

Central Idea: The two major reasons genetically engineered crops pose serious dangers to the environment and to human health are that are being implanted with conglomerations of genes from viruses, bacteria, insects, and animals, and organic crops are being polluted with the pollen from gene-altered plants destroying the purity of organic.

Questions of Value

Persuasive presentations that address questions of value focus on the worth we attach to an idea or action. Moreover, this type of persuasive presentation calls upon the audience to make a judgment as to the worth of an idea or action. Usually the presenter seeks to persuade the audience that something is good or bad or right or wrong. However, many times the speaker seeks to compare by persuading the audience that something is better than something else or the best option. A **topical** pattern of organization is best suited to persuasive presentations designed to address questions of value. The main points in the body of your presentation should be the reasons it is good or bad, right or wrong, or better or the best.

Specific Purpose: To persuade the members of the American Bar Association who are present that capital punishment is morally and legally wrong.

Central Idea: The four major reasons capital punishment is morally and legally wrong are that it does not act as a deterrent for crime, it is irreversible and could be used on an innocent person, it is more expensive than imprisonment, and it encourages revenge over rehabilitation.

Specific Purpose: To persuade members of the American Medical Association who are present that swimming is the ideal form of cardiovascular exercise.

Central Idea: The two major reasons swimming is the ideal form of cardiovascular exerciseare that it works more muscle groups than any single form of exercise and is easier on a person's joints.

Questions of Policy

Persuasive presentations that address questions of policy focus on change. When delivering a question of policy presentation, you must decide whether your goal is to gain passive agreement or to stimulate immediate action.

There are two major organizational patterns that are appropriate for a question of policy presentation. A **problem-solution** pattern of organization uses two main points. The first is the problem(s), or why change is needed, and the second is the solution(s), or what you are proposing. In addition, a sequential pattern known as **Monroe's Motivational Sequence** is the recommended pattern to use, because it follows a logical pattern of thought and ensures that you include all aspects in your persuasive message. This pattern will be discussed below. In both of these patterns the reasons are not main points, but are the subpoints under the first main point in the body.

Question of Policy to Gain Passive Agreement

Specific Purpose: To persuade the members of the NCAA legislative assembly that college scholarship athletes should receive a $250 monthly stipend for personal expenses.

Central Idea (Problem-Solution):

Today I will discuss the reasons college scholarship athletes should receive a $250 monthly stipend for personal expenses, and how this will work.

Specific Purpose: To persuade members of the legislative assembly for the National Education Association that affirmative-action programs be eliminated by college admissions offices.

Central Idea (Monroe's Motivational Sequence):

Today I will show you the reasons affirmative-action programs should be eliminated by college admissions offices, alternatives to affirmative action, and the benefits to eliminating these programs for college admissions.

Question of Policy to Gain Immediate Action

Specific Purpose: To persuade members of the National Retail Association to boycott clothing made at sweatshops.

Central Idea (Problem-Solution):

Today I will show you the reasons you should boycott clothing made at sweatshops, and alternatives to buying these clothes.

Specific Purpose: To persuade members of Student Government Association to donate time to Habitat for Humanity.

Central Idea (Monroe's Motivational Sequence):

Today, I will discuss the reasons your time is needed, how you can volunteer, and the benefits of volunteering your time to Habitat for Humanity.

Monroe's Motivational Sequence

Monroe's Motivational Sequence is popular with many speakers because it offers a clear series of steps to follow when developing and delivering a persuasive message.[32] It should only be used for persuasive presentations on question of policy. The five steps include attention, need, satisfaction, visualization, and action. The advantage of using this sequence is that it provides listeners with a clearly structured message that tends to follow the way receivers process messages. Below are the five steps to Monroe's Motivational Sequence, the purpose of each step, and where each step is found in your presentation.

1. **Attention** (introduction). You must first gain the attention and interest of your listeners in the introduction of your presentation.

2. **Need** (first main point in body). During the need step, you must explain the reasons change is needed. The speaker must convince the audience that there is a serious problem with the existing situation that requires this change. It is important to relate to values and experiences of the audience during the need phase of the presentation. In addition, it is in this portion of the presentation that you will answer most audience objections.

3. **Satisfaction** (second main point in body). In the satisfaction phase of the presentation, you will propose solution(s) to the problem(s) identified in the need phase of the presentation. You will present an in-depth plan in this phase to make clear how and why the plan would work.

4. **Visualization** (third main point in body). Benefits are explained in this step by showing what will be improved if your solution is adopted. You will also use analogical reasoning in this phase to illustrate how your solution has worked in a similar situation. If you are attempting to gain passive agreement, you will explain exactly how this change can and would be made (how it works).

If you are attempting to gain immediate action, it will be necessary to explain how to do it, who to contact, where to go, etc. If asking your audience to refrain from doing something (change), this section should focus on providing the audience with alternatives to this behavior.

5. **Action** (conclusion). Now that the audience knows the benefits of your plan, you will need to remind them of what needs to be done or what you want them to do. During this phase of the presentation, tell them who to contact, where to go, and how to take action.

Building Persuasive Arguments

There are a number of actions that you can take to build strong persuasive arguments. Earlier we reviewed the delivery factors that will help you build and convey effective messages. In this section, we focus on the factors that make a difference to the target audience and will help you build and convey effective persuasive messages. We will group these factors by source, message, and receiver.

When considering **source factors**, our interest centers on the "things" about the source that may make a difference to receivers. When receivers are presented with persuasive messages, what impact (if any) will source characteristics have on whether or not the persuasive message is accepted or rejected by the receivers? The following factors about the source make a difference to the receiver of a persuasive appeal:

*   **Source credibility**. Credibility is the factor that makes the single greatest difference to receivers. Receivers evaluate the credibility of a source in two ways. The lesson for speakers is to do all you can (within accepted ethical bounds) to influence how receivers judge your competence and trustworthiness.

*   **Competence**. Receivers make judgments about competence in terms of the speaker's expertise with the topic. Receivers' judgments of expertise are tied to the speaker's experience with the topic, position in an organization, level of education, awards and honors received, etc.

*   **Trustworthiness**. Trust is developed over time, as well as through the reputation the speaker enjoys with members of the audience and their network. These judgments of competence and trust work in tandem, so it is essential that speakers seek to be judged highly in both regards.

Building Credibility

Are you a credible source of information? As we noted, receivers assess source credibility in terms of competence and trustworthiness. Based on this information, what can you do? Competence and trustworthiness are not easy to establish, especially with an unfamiliar audience. Interestingly, there are several actions that you can take to positively influence how the audience assesses your competence and trustworthiness.

- To begin, make sure that you are prepared! Nothing substitutes for preparation in business communication. Your level of preparation will convey to the audience your knowledge and expertise of the topic. Lack of preparation generally translates into negative assessments of knowledge and expertise.

- Seek to establish your credentials (competence) in the introduction. This can be accomplished by providing the audience with information about yourself (e.g., education level, previous experience with the topic, professional credentials, colleagues with whom you have worked, etc.) that will separate you from others who have little or no knowledge of the topic.

- Whenever possible, stress the commonalities that you share with audience members. Not surprisingly, people with similar experiences tend to be viewed more positively than people with whom we have little in common.

- Make use of two-sided arguments whenever possible in persuasive presentations. Speakers who make use of two-sided arguments are perceived by listeners as more objective and trustworthy than speakers who focus exclusively on one side of an issue. You need to do this so it will not seem as if you are trying to hide anything from your audience.

In addition to source credibility, the following factors about the source make a difference to the receiver of a persuasive appeal:

- **Liking**. If the source is perceived as likeable, he or she is viewed more positively by receivers.

- **Similarity**. If the source is perceived as being similar to listeners, he or she is viewed more positively by receivers.

- **Physical attractiveness**. If the source is perceived as physically attractive, it is viewed more positively by receivers.

Receiver Factors

When considering receiver factors, our interest centers on the internal qualities or characteristics of a person that influences his or her reaction to persuasive appeals. Much of this research focused on whether males or females are more easily persuaded. Contrary to popular opinion, there are no differences between females and males in regards to the likelihood of either accepting or rejecting a speaker's persuasive appeals. Early research in persuasion suggested that women were more easily persuaded than men. However, it is now clear that access to power (and not gender) is the factor that makes a difference. Simply put, those in positions of power are *generally* less susceptible to persuasion than those in lesser positions of power. As a speaker, learn to recognize who in the audience holds power and authority. Other receiver factors, such as dogmatism (stubbornness), do not appear to have a clear impact on the acceptance or rejection of persuasive appeals.

Message Factors

When considering message factors, our interest centers on the "things" that can be done to a message that may make a difference in whether receivers accept or reject a persuasive appeal. For example, messages vary (or can be modified) in terms of organization and content.

- **Organizing the arguments**. Persuasive messages often include more than one appeal. The speaker will use several different appeals or arguments to influence the attitudes/behaviors of receivers. When multiple persuasive appeals are used, is it more effective to put your best persuasive appeal first, last, or in the middle of a presentation? In general, it appears that the best answer is to start or end with your strongest appeal. There does not appear to be a benefit to placing the best appeal in the middle of the series of appeals. The situation (Do you have limited time? Has everyone arrived?) should influence your thinking about whether to start or end with your strongest persuasive appeal. In other instances, the organization of your arguments may be influenced by the amount of background information that the audience requires to understand the appeal. For example, if you are making a persuasive argument involving the rebuilding of New Orleans, the audience may need to be informed of what the current levee system is designed to do. Thus, that informative content may influence how you organize your arguments.

- **Message content**. Messages can be modified in numerous ways. Research suggests the following about the content of persuasive messages:

  - Recommendations to the audience must be clear. If the audience is uncertain about what you want them to believe and/ or do, it is unlikely you will achieve your objectives.

  - Two-sided arguments are better than one-sided arguments. When a speaker presents several different viewpoints followed by an explanation as to why he/she believes one to be the best, receivers view the source as more credible and competent. In the eyes of the audience, this kind of appeal suggests the speaker knows the issues and has considered more than one option. To do this, you need to mention the opposing argument and immediately counteract it with your argument. You may say, for example, "I know that you may be thinking that… (opposing argument). However, … (evidence for your argument)."

- Fear appeals work only as long as the receiver remains fearful. Fear tends to be a short-term state for most people. If you rely on fear appeals, the message must accomplish two ends. First, it must induce sustained fear in the audience. Second, it must not make them so fearful that they are unable to act.

- When seeking to change existing attitudes or behaviors, the messages that are most effective are judged by receivers as advocating a position that is *moderately* different than the one currently held by receivers. If the message calls for very little change, receivers tend not to see the need for any action on their part. If the message calls for great change, receivers tend to resist the message because of the magnitude of the change. A message that calls for moderate change (in the eyes of the receivers) tends to be most effective.

- **Using evidence**. Speakers can make use of evidence in persuasive messages in a variety of ways. However, not all ways of using evidence are equally effective. Speakers use evidence to help support or refute a persuasive appeal. When using evidence in a persuasive presentation, consider the following:

  - Anticipate the objections listeners might have to the evidence (e.g., it is dated, the evidence comes from a single study, the source of the evidence is questionable, etc.) and prepare to overcome those objections with additional evidence (if possible). If you anticipate that the audience members have objections to the purpose that your evidence cannot overcome, you may need to revisit the purpose of the presentation.

  - Make use of specific evidence that is relevant to members of *this* audience, rather than the population in general. As stated before, audience analysis is even more important in a persuasive presentation because you are dealing with people's beliefs, values, behaviors, etc.

  - Make use of novel (new), interesting evidence that generates a lasting impression. If your listeners have heard the same arguments before and have not changed their minds or behaviors, chances are hearing them in your presentation will not create change. So, research carefully to find information that will create new arguments.

  - Make clear how the evidence is related to the purpose of the presentation. All evidence must directly relate to the specific purpose and each argument you are making. In your presentation, you will need to explain its relevance.

Reasoning

For the purposes of this course, we will define **reasoning** as the way people draw conclusions from the available information and evidence. We reason every day to better understand and explain why things happen. Reasoning impacts persuasive speaking in two ways. First, the speaker develops a persuasive appeal that is based on some form of reasoning. Second, receivers employ reasoning in the process of accepting or rejecting a persuasive appeal. Thus, the way you and your audience reason will impact the extent to which you achieve your objectives. As a persuasive speaker, it is essential that you convince audience members to agree with your line of reasoning. In this course, you must become familiar with four methods of reasoning.

- **Causal reasoning**. When individuals use causal reasoning, they draw the conclusion that a cause (often the presence of something or some act) leads to a specific effect or set of effects. For example, a driver involved in a minor accident might conclude that the presence of water on the road caused his car to leave the road and drop into a ditch. The driver might further reason that if the cause (the water on the road) had not been present, the effect (running off the road into a ditch) would not have occurred.

  - Because the other product got to market first, you have not considered our product.

  - Our customers were unhappy with service options. So, I've changed them.

- **Analogical reasoning**. When individuals employ analogical reasoning, they draw conclusions based on comparisons. For example, if you are a great communicator, you would make a great attorney. Reasoning by comparison suggests that many things in our world are believed to be associated. In a question of policy presentation, you will need to use analogical reasoning to show your audience where a similar plan to yours has worked successfully (visualization step in Monroe's Motivated Sequence).

  - At Dell, the distribution process takes less than three days. Surely we can do the same with our distribution network.

  - Many have already enrolled in this program and benefited greatly. If it can work for them, it can work for you too.

- **Reasoning from specific instance.** The use of this type of reasoning suggests that a person is making use of specific facts to draw a much broader conclusion about others or events in the world. You must find the conclusion that is being drawn in the statement. It could come in the beginning or end, but it will be very general and vague.

  - Pollution is present in the Tennessee River at Knoxville. Pollution is present in the Tennessee River at Chattanooga. Therefore, the Tennessee River is polluted.

  - Our product was in the customer's hand when the job was completed. It looks like our product got the job done.

- **Reasoning from principle.** This type of reasoning suggests that a person applies a general premise (principle) to arrive at a very specific conclusion. For the most part, reasoning from principle lacks the hard facts found in reasoning from specific instance. However, many times it will include a three-fold statement that begins with a general principle, followed by a minor premise that may resemble a fact, and ends with a specific conclusion. Again, no matter what the wording, the conclusion is what you must find. If it is very specific in nature, it is reasoning from principle.

  - People in this industry have the inside track to the top. You will probably be a top player, like others before you.

  - Politicians who are guilty of corruption do not deserve to be reelected. Last year our U.S. Representative was found to be using campaign donations for personal finance gain. Therefore, our U.S. Representatives do not deserve to be reelected.

In the second example, separate the components of the message and observe what is included:

Premise → Fact → Specific Conclusion

All forms of reasoning have limitations. How would you describe the limitations of the four methods of reasoning described above? If you are unsure what the limitations are, consider the following:

- Causal reasoning is limited to the extent that we have identified accurately the cause(s) that lead to specific effects.

- Analogical reasoning is limited to the extent that comparisons hold true. If people enjoy business-to-business sales, does that mean they will enjoy door-to-door sales?

- Reasoning from a specific instance is limited to the extent that facts from several specific instances can be applied to a more general class of events or others. In other words, because the information is true in two or three instances, is it true in all or most all instances?

- Reasoning from a principle is limited to the extent that we can apply a broad idea or principle to a specific instance. In other words, because we conclude that the information is true in most all cases, is it true in this case?

Effective presenters tend to be more aware of the limitations associated with each type of reasoning, and are cautious about how they make use of reasoning in the development of persuasive presentations. Far too often, however, speakers employ incorrect reasoning or reasoning that is not sound in a persuasive presentation. A **fallacy** involves errors in reasoning. For the purpose of this course, we have identified eight fallacies that you should guard against:

- **Hasty generalization**. This type of reasoning error occurs when a speaker jumps to a general conclusion on the basis of poorly selected specific facts. To avoid this, seek out other evidence such as statistics or testimony to support your broad conclusion.

- **Mistaken cause**. For all of us, one experience is always followed by other experiences. Reasoning errors involving mistaken causes occur when a speaker erroneously assumes that the first event/experience must have caused the second event/experience.

- **Invalid analogy**. An invalid analogy takes place when a speaker uses fallacious reasoning to suggest similarities in two cases when they are truly different.

- **Red herring**. Speakers seeking to divert attention from the issue at hand often engage in fallacious reasoning by introducing irrelevant issues into the topic of discussion.

- *ad hominem* (Latin for "*against the man*"). Simply put, a speaker uses fallacious reasoning by attacking the messenger rather than the message or idea that is in dispute.

- **False dilemma**. A false dilemma involves a situation where the speaker uses fallacious reasoning to force listeners to choose between only two alternatives when more than two alternatives exist. It is usually presented as an ultimatum.

- **Bandwagon**. Bandwagon reasoning is fallacious because it does not concern the soundness of an idea. This form of fallacious reasoning is based on the notion that because something is popular it is therefore correct, good, or desired.

- **Slippery slope**. Conclusions that are based on an illogical chain of events often involve slippery slope reasoning. A speaker engaging in slippery slope reasoning assumes that the first step will be followed by other steps that cannot be prevented.

Emotional Appeal

Since the work of Aristotle, study and instruction in communication suggest that emotion plays a key role in persuasive presentations. This view is grounded in the idea that people are more likely to change attitudes or behaviors when their passions are stirred. In your persuasive presentations, you may consider making the audience feel sad, proud, angry, sympathetic, fearful, etc., to further influence them. The key is to *never* substitute emotional appeal for evidence or reasoning, but use it in addition to solid evidence and reasoning.

MANAGING RECEIVER EMOTIONS

Effective persuasive speakers recognize the importance of managing the emotions of the receivers. There is no single method to ensure that, as a business communicator, you generate the desired emotional response in receivers. However, the following factors are often used to influence emotional states of listeners:

- **Language use**. Vivid, descriptive language is often used to elicit emotional responses from the audience. Often this is accomplished in the form of an example, story, or personal experience.

- **Nonverbal messages**. Facial expressions and body movement convey to an audience the mood the presenter is attempting to establish.

- **Use of voice**. Volume and pitch are used by business communicators to convey more than content. Your voice can be managed through the use of volume, vocal variety, and pauses.

Persuasive presenters often employ appeals that are based, in part, on managing the emotional state of the receivers in terms of fear, anger, or sympathy. While the emotional states of receivers are important in persuasive presentations, consider the following:

- The effects of emotion on attitudes or behaviors tend to persist as long as the emotional state persists. When the receiver gets over the feelings of fear or hatred or happiness, the effects on attitudes tend to go away.

- How ethical is it to make others angry or guilty or fearful? Are there situations where it would be both appropriate and ethical to generate strong emotions in receivers? Are there instances where it is inappropriate? When answering this, consider the major rule above. One way that emotional appeal is abused is when a persuasive presentation relies solely on emotional appeals and uses them as a substitute for evidence and reasoning. This is not only unethical, but your audience will recognize your attempt to take advantage of them.

Group Presentations

Group presentations are common in many different kinds of organizations. In particular, organizations that arrange work activities around teams make use of group presentations. Group presentations offer a number of advantages over individual presentations but may potentially involve disadvantages. First, a group of individuals brings more resources to the task. That is, groups enjoy a greater range of skills, more collective knowledge, and an overall advantage in the collective time that can be devoted to the task. Second, group members are able to divide tasks and, as a result, concentrate efforts on each of the component parts of the presentation. The potential costs involved in a group presentation are twofold: the challenge of coordinating the activities of two or more people and social loafing (relying on others in the group to do the work).

Although group presentations share many of the characteristics of other types of presentations, there are several factors that make this type of presentation unique. Specifically, those factors include:

- Organizing the work-related tasks. Typically, groups organize in terms of the specific tasks that must be completed or they bring their assigned role to the group.

- Developing and maintaining group cohesion. Groups constitute social systems and, as a result, group members must be able to maintain working relationships in order to complete the presentation.

- Groups receive collective rewards (or punishments) for the presentation rather than individual rewards.

In addition to the factors described above, the delivery of the group presentation has several special conditions associated with it. Specifically, effective group presentations require that all group members:

- be introduced to the audience.

- appear interested and involved with the presentation throughout the entire event.

- are prepared to assist other members in the event of an unexpected difficulty with visual aids, etc.

- be prepared to deal with question-and-answer sessions at the end of the presentation.

- dress appropriately and arrive in a timely manner for the presentation.

Special Occasion Presentations

Many special occasions call for different types of presentations. Your decision about the type of presentation to deliver in the special event will be determined by factors such as the purpose of the event, its location, and the composition of the audience.

There are five main types of special occasion presentations. For many special occasions, more than one type of presentation may be appropriate. Special occasion presentations differ considerably from informative or persuasive presentations in that special occasion presentations most often seek to accomplish the general goal of **entertainment**.

ALL SPECIAL OCCASION PRESENTATIONS

No matter the type of special occasion, the following criteria will be useful in preparing for the presentation:

- **Be creative**. Exercise your creativity when preparing and delivering this type of presentation. You can do this by bringing visual aids/props that will make your audience feel that they are part of this special event.

- **Adapt to the occasion**. Your presentation will depend greatly on the type of event and location of this event. Is it a small, informal company barbecue, or a large, company-wide formal banquet? What is the appropriate attire at this event? Often, situational factors of the occasion will give you clues as to how to proceed. An informal event will call for less formal language and delivery than a formal event. Based on where your event is, you may need a podium for a formal occasion or you may be expected to stand out in front of your audience in less formal occasions. In the introduction, make clear why we are here.

- **Adapt to the audience**. Consider who would be at this event and how they will define the situation (celebration, farewell gathering, etc.).

- **Organize material effectively**. Organizational patterns for this type of presentation tend to vary, but most often topical and chronological patterns are employed to organize the material.

- **Use clear/vivid language**. The language used in this presentation needs to be both clear and vivid since you will be seeking to evoke responses in the audience and, as a result, inspire them or bid farewell to a colleague.

- **Maintain strong eye contact**. Eye contact is even more important for special occasion presentations, because most events call for less formality than many business-related informative or persuasive presentations.

- **Use voice/body effectively**. This type of presentation must not be delivered in a monotone voice with few gestures. Remember, this is a special occasion!

PRESENTATION TO INTRODUCE

One type of special occasion presentation has as a goal to introduce a person. It may be to introduce the main speaker or performer at an event, or it may be to introduce a new organization member, client, etc. Consider the following guidelines when preparing the introduction:

- **Build enthusiasm for the upcoming speaker/performer**. You want the audience to become excited to see and hear the person/group whom you are introducing. One way you can do this is by giving your audience information that they may not have ever heard about this person/group. Be creative in finding information. Consider including achievements, personal struggles, family, etc. When doing this, consider your audience. The main way that you can build enthusiasm for the upcoming speaker is to wait and reveal the speaker's/performer's name at the *end* of the presentation. There will be times that the content of your presentation gives the audience clues as to whom you are introducing, but the person's name is saved for the concluding sentence.

- **Build enthusiasm for the speaker's topic**. Not only will you need to include content about the speaker/performer, you also must be specific about what this person/group is coming to do. If you are introducing a speaker, you should tell the audience what topic he or she plans to address.

- **Establish a welcoming climate that will boost the speaker's credibility**. For this presentation, it is important that you include information that awards the presenter the level of credibility appropriate for that audience. Depending on who you are introducing, your remarks to boost their credibility may differ. However, regardless of whom you are introducing, avoid statements that might embarrass the person.

- **Make sure your remarks are completely accurate**. When gathering information for the presentation, make sure that the dates are correct, the stories are true, and the events are factually correct. Your credibility as a speaker and the person's credibility may be reduced by inaccurate information.

- **Adapt your remarks to the audience**. When considering what to include in your speech and how to deliver it, think about your audience. Who will be at this event? What would they already know about the person being introduced? What would they be interested in hearing or learning about this person?

- **Create a sense of anticipation and drama**. You can do this in the same way in which you built enthusiasm for the upcoming speaker. For example, leave the person's name for the concluding statement.

- **Adhere to time limits**. Remember that the audience did not come to this event to see you, but rather to see the speaker. Therefore, the presentation should be much shorter than other types of presentations.

COMMEMORATIVE PRESENTATION

The purpose of a commemorative presentation is to inspire the audience by paying tribute to a person, a group of people, an institution, or an idea. This event usually represents a milestone in someone's life, such as a retirement gathering, or an organizational milestone, such as the closing of an old facility or a groundbreaking ceremony.

- **Effective introduction.** You should begin your commemorative presentation with an introduction that gains attention first, and is followed by the introduction of the person or the occasion involved in the tribute.

- **Supporting material that inspires.** Because your purpose is to inspire the audience, you need to find material that meets that goal. Vivid language is important to inspire the audience as well as evoke their emotions.

- **Effective conclusion.** Just as you would in an informative or persuasive presentation, it is necessary to end with a vivid, memorable statement that culminates with the overall theme of the event. Remember, end with a bang!

AFTER-DINNER PRESENTATION

The purpose of an after-dinner presentation is to entertain the audience by making a thoughtful point about a topic in a lighthearted manner. These presentations do not have to be made after dinner or even relate to meals or food. This type of special occasion presentation is consistent with other persuasive or informative presentations in terms of structure and organization. However, the principle goal is to entertain your audience. The following guidelines will assist you in preparing for the after-dinner presentation:

- **Choose an appropriate topic for the audience.** When approaching this kind of event, select a topic appropriate for the audience and the occasion. Remember, the audience is there to be entertained!

- **The introduction.** Just as in a commemorative presentation, you should begin your after-dinner presentation with an introduction that gains attention first and introduces your topic/purpose. It should also include any welcome that you wish to offer individuals in the audience or the group.

- **The supporting material.** Since the purpose is to entertain, you need to gather information for the presentation that meets this goal. Research the topic to find its "lighter side." You are looking for interesting information that will keep the audience's attention.

- **Use tasteful humor.** Not surprisingly, humor is often used in after-dinner presentations. Make use of humor if it comes naturally to you and it is not something that you have to force. If humor does not come naturally to you, the audience may feel uncomfortable with its use and be uncertain as to whether or not they should laugh. When using humor, make certain that your target audience will find it tasteful; people are not entertained when they are offended!

- **The conclusion**. Just as with informative and persuasive presentations, it is necessary to end with a vivid, memorable statement that captures the overall theme of your presentation. Remember to end the presentation with a bang!

Presenting/Accepting Awards

Events in which a speaker presents an award or bestows recognition frequently take place in organizations. This presentation is usually shorter than other types of special occasion presentations, since awards to individuals are often given to individuals in the context of a larger banquet designed to recognize many different people. In this situation, the goal is to offer a brief, vivid account of why the person is receiving the award.

The purpose of an acceptance presentation is to thank members of the organization for the gift or award. This may include thanking the person(s) who presented you with the award, as well as the people that helped to make it possible. Moreover, this type of presentation is relatively brief for the reasons described above.

Key Terms

Informative presentations

Persuasive presentations

Persuasion defined

Attitudes

Target audience

Types of persuasive presentations

Monroe's Motivational Sequence

Source factors

Receiver factors

Message factors

Building credibility

Using evidence

Reasoning

Fallacy

Emotional appeals

Special occasion presentations

ENDNOTES

30. O'Keefe, D.J. (2002). *Persuasion: Theory and research* (2nd ed.). Thousand Oaks, CA: Sage.

31. Shavitt, S., & Brock, T.C. (1994). *Persuasion: Psychological insights and perspectives*. Needham Heights, MA: Allyn & Bacon.

32. McKerrow, R.E., Gronbeck, B.E., Ehninger, D., & Monroe, A.H. (2000). *Principles and types of speech communication* (14th ed.). New York: Addison Wesley.

CHAPTER 8

USING LANGUAGE

Overview

Language may be viewed as a resource that business communicators use to convey ideas. Regrettably, not every person is equally skillful in the use of language when delivering presentations. The goal for this chapter is to advance your understanding of the role of language in business presentations and to build your skills in using language.

Language and Business Presentations

In a sense, speakers work with a "set of tools" to achieve their objectives. The set of tools that you will use to "construct" a presentation includes visual aids, body movement, supporting information, and the pattern of organizing that you will use for your message. All of these items are used by the speaker to achieve his/her objectives. Moreover, the speaker can polish his/her skills with each of these elements. A very important instrument in the speaker's toolbox involves language.

Language may be thought of as a symbol system through which we create and exchange meanings. Language use is governed by a set of rules that speakers are expected to follow. For example, we have rules about how people are expected to initiate conversations as well as how people should conclude conversations. We have rules that involve turn-taking in conversations. Quite literally, there are hundreds of rules that govern the way we use language.

The rules for language use are prescriptive. That is, the rules lay out for us what we are expected to do when we use language. The rules for public speaking situations in the business world vary a bit from the rules that govern language use in conversations. For example, our day-to-day conversations are governed by turn-taking rules. It is a violation of the rules for language use for one person to do all the talking while others do all of the listening. In presentation situations,

In Chapter Eight, you will learn about:

- What Language Is and the Four Language Rules

- The Difference Between Denotative and Connotative Meaning

- How to Use Rhythmic Devices

that rule for turn-taking is different. In this situation, we expect one party to do most all of the talking and all others to do most all of the listening. Although a vast number of rules exist that govern our use of language, we will focus our attention on four rules or maxims that you will be expected to follow. The four rules will be referred to as quality, quantity, relation, and clarity.

- **Clarity**. The clarity rule suggests that speakers should avoid ambiguity. That is, a speaker should not use language that is vague or unclear when communicating with others. Use terminology that your specific audience will understand. While being professional and adapting to your audience, be sure to use terms that you feel comfortable using.

- **Relation**. The relation rule suggests that speakers should make clear the connections between their ideas. Use specific language that directly makes the connection through explanation. Do not make the audience figure out the relationship between the ideas that are discussed in your speech on their own. Rather, seek to manage how the audience should view the relationship between your ideas. How do you respond to speakers when they engage in a series of topic shifts about topics that do not appear to be related?

- **Quality**. The quality rule suggests that we should tell the truth as we know it. You can do this by reporting your information accurately as you find it. Do not paraphrase ideas to such an extent that it does not resemble the original information. As a speaker, when (if ever) is it acceptable to violate the quality rule?

- **Quantity**. The quantity rule suggests that speakers should say no more and no less than what is needed to convey a message. How do audience members communicate to speakers that the quantity rule is being violated? Many students will use four or five sentences to say what he or she could have explained in one or two. Because of this, presentations often go over the time allotted. The way to condense the material in your presentation to avoid violating this rule is to **eliminate clutter**. To do this effectively, complete your preparation outline. After it is completed, go back and take out words, phrases, or sentences that are not necessary. Often, you will need to eliminate unnecessary adjectives or synonyms.

Clearly, there are times when we violate the rules that speakers are expected to follow. For example, when trying to persuade an audience that is hostile to your purpose, it makes sense to defer your purpose statement until late in the presentation. In this situation, you would violate the rule on clarity. Audience members will judge your performance, in part, on the extent to which you conform to the rules for business communication. Consider carefully any decision to violate the rules.

Language is a very powerful tool that allows speakers to convey meanings to listeners. Since language involves a system of symbols, speakers must be cautious about the meanings that receivers assign to symbols. Simply put, a **symbol** may be thought of as one thing

standing for something else. The wildly popular use of :) in email messages symbolizes or stands for a smiling face. However, it might be interpreted as meaning agreement, I am happy, I am happy with you, etc. Since the meanings we assign to symbols are not always clear, business communicators must consider how receivers are likely to understand and interpret the symbols (verbal and nonverbal messages, visual aids, etc.) used in a presentation.

Language and Meaning

Language is used by speakers to define the situation. That is, speakers use messages to shape the way listeners come to understand what is going on around them. For example, does this situation present us with an opportunity or a problem? Does this situation involve work, or should it be understood as play? Not surprisingly, receivers do not always accept how speakers define the situation through their language use. However, skillful language use does provide the speaker with a powerful tool to shape the way listeners view the world around them. When interpreting the meaning of language, receivers employ the following practices:

- **Denotative meanings**. Denotative meanings involve the literal meaning of a word or phrase. It is the dictionary definition of the term. Thus, the denotative meaning of the word "cool" to a receiver involves chilly temperatures.

- **Connotative meanings**. The connotative meaning of a word or phrase is more subjective. Connotative meanings extend beyond the literal meaning of a word and are subject to interpretation by speakers and listeners. It usually evokes some sort of emotion in the listener. For example, the connotative meaning of "cool" may be that an individual or event is viewed positively. However, if the speaker uses the word "cool" in sarcastic fashion, it may mean that the individual or event is viewed negatively. As a speaker, it is important to recognize that the members of your audience may vary in the connotative meanings that they assign to your message.

Appropriate Use of Language

When preparing and delivering presentations, keep in mind the following tips concerning language:

- **Be clear**. If the audience is uncertain as to the meaning of your message, you will not achieve your objectives.

- **Be accurate**. Inaccurate messages will diminish your credibility in the eyes of the receivers.

- **Be memorable**. Use language in such a way that your message is unforgettable. You can achieve the goal of creating memorable messages by using language to bring issues into sharp focus or bringing together ideas in a novel way. For example, the message, "Ask not what your country can do for you; ask what you can do for your country" created a lasting memory for listeners, because two different ideas were brought together in a novel way.

- **Be creative**. Use creative, vivid words and phrases to generate and maintain interest in the message.

When preparing and delivering presentations, you should avoid the following ways of using language:

- **Biased language**. Language that reflects a bias against or toward individuals on the basis of gender, race, religion, or background is unacceptable. In fact, according to the credo used in this course, it is unethical.

- **Culturally insensitive language**. Language that is not sensitive to cultural differences is unacceptable. According to the credo used in this course, it is unethical.

- **Cliché**. Such overused expressions as "dry as a bone," "nice guys finish last," and "sharp as a tack" are to be avoided in presentations, because they do not add much to the message or suggest original thinking on the part of the speaker. Information that is not new will not capture the attention of the audience. Do you know someone who uses too many clichés on a regular basis? Do you like to listen to that person in conversation?

Vivid Language

One way to make your message memorable is make use of vivid language. **Vivid language** produces distinct mental images in the receivers. With the language that you select to make the presentation, you paint a picture for the audience. The "picture" is most readily understood by receivers when the speaker uses:

- **Concrete vs. abstract words**. Concrete language enables the audience to create a mental picture of a real, tangible item, creating **imagery**. For example: "West Town Mall" is concrete; "retail shopping area" is abstract.

- **Descriptive language**. Descriptive language adds detail to the mental image in the mind of the receiver. Simply put, descriptive language involves the use of adjectives or adverbs to add greater depth and clarity to the message. This gives the audience a chance to understand more clearly the picture that you are depicting.

- **Intense language**. Language intensity adds strength and power to the message. For example, stating that a concert was great or inspiring captures the attention of an audience much more readily than saying that it was a "good" concert.

- **Comparisons**. Business communicators often use comparisons to help their audience better understand their ideas.

  - **Metaphor**. This involves thinking about or experiencing one thing in terms of another, usually by comparing them. For example, life is a journey. Thinking about life as a journey offers a number of opportunities for speakers to make use of concepts associated with a journey, such as bumps in the road, growth as a result of new experiences, etc.

  - **Simile**. This is similar to a metaphor, except it compares the two items using the words "like" or "as." For example, life is like a journey.

- **Rhythmic devices**. Speakers often make use of rhythm in their presentations to create an appealing sound to the listener.

  - **Antithesis**. This is when the speaker pairs opposites. For example, Charles Dickens wrote in his novel *A Tale of Two Cities*: It was the best of times; it was the worst of times. Another example involves the inaugural speech of John F. Kennedy, when he stated, "Ask not what your country can do for you; ask what you can do for your country."

  - **Parallelism**. This is when you use a similar pair or series of words, phrases, or sentences that sometimes uses repetition. For example, "I speak as a Republican. I speak as a woman. I speak as a United States Senator. I speak as an American." (Margaret Chase Smith)

  - **Alliteration**. This is the repetition of phonetic sounds, usually consonant sounds, at the beginning of words or phrases. For example, "In a nation founded on the promise of human dignity, our colleges, our communities, our country should challenge hatred wherever we find it." (Hillary Rodham Clinton)

Key Terms

Language

Language rules

  Clarity

  Relation

  Quality

  Quantity

Denotative meanings

Connotative meanings

Appropriate language use

Vivid language

Rhythmic devices

Unit Three will introduce you to basic communication skills involving interpersonal, group, and team interaction.

CHAPTER 9
Introduces the reader to the skills necessary to develop effective working relationships.

CHAPTER 10
Introduces the reader to the skills necessary to be successful in a diverse workplace.

CHAPTER 11
Introduces the reader to the skills necessary for effective work group interaction.

CHAPTER 12
Introduces the reader to the skills associated with effective communication in the group decision-making process.

UNIT 3

CHAPTER 9

DEVELOPING EFFECTIVE
WORKPLACE RELATIONSHIPS

Overview

Developing effective workplace relationships is essential for career success. Each member of an organization operates in a web of relationships through which job duties and responsibilities are carried out. Depending on the organization and your specific job, you may potentially develop workplace relationships across a broad spectrum of people that may include supervisors, co-workers, clients and customers, government officials, and members of other organizations with whom you regularly interact (e.g., UPS delivery person, copier service person, and a variety of sales/marketing representatives). While you are likely to be aware of the wide-ranging kinds of relationships people experience in the workplace, you may not question why we enter into relationships or how they evolve. Moreover, most people understand that effective relationships are important in the workplace, but may be less clear on how to actually build effective relationships. Our goal in this chapter is to introduce the reader to the skills necessary to develop effective working relationships.

As we noted earlier, people in organizations communicate in order to achieve objectives. Similarly, when people establish relationships in the work world, they do so in order to meet objectives and/or needs. Building effective relationships is a challenge, regardless of whether you are initiating a new business relationship or maintaining an existing relationship. Not surprisingly, initiating a relationship presents a different set of communication challenges than seeking to maintain a relationship. However, in both instances, we seek to meet a set of communication objectives (e.g., functional goals, relational goals, and identity management goals). Since the inception of the Human Relations Movement, we have come to recognize that people have social needs (e.g., a sense of belonging) that may be met through workplace relationships.

In Chapter Nine, you will learn about:

- Developing Effective Workplace Relationships

- Dimensions of Relationships

- Interpersonal Communication in Organizations

  - Supervisor-Subordinate Communication

  - Peer Relationships

  - Sexual Harassment

The nature and quality of a relationship may be influenced by a variety of factors. In business settings, several factors or dimensions of a relationship are particularly impactful. These dimensions include power and status, attraction, involvement, and the situation.[33]

Dimensions of Relationships

Power and status refers to the ability of an individual to exert influence over others.[34] People vary in terms of the amount of power they hold in an organization. No person in an organization is without power but because of the hierarchical nature of organizations, some people have more influence than others. Our thinking about power in co-worker relationships has been strongly influenced by the work of French and Raven, beginning in the 1950s. These scholars identified five bases from which people draw power: referent, expert, legitimate, coercive, and reward power. Although this work was initially published more than 50 years ago, current research continues to support these five bases for power in workplace relationships.[35]

- **Referent** power is viewed as the extent to which a person is liked by others. Those possessing high levels of referent power are admired by others for their personal qualities, and others often seek to be like this person.

- **Expert** power is viewed as the extent to which a person is perceived as possessing extensive knowledge or expertise in a subject/activity.

- **Legitimate** power is viewed as influence that stems from a code or standard of conduct. In a business setting, that code will include the formal authority granted to a person because of his/her position (e.g., manager).

- **Coercive** power is viewed as the extent to which a person is capable of punishing or withholding benefits from others.

- **Reward** power is viewed as the extent to which a person is capable of awarding benefits to others.

An individual's level of **attraction** is often assumed to be linked to physical characteristics. It is certainly true that physical attractiveness is a factor in whether individuals seek to establish a relationship with other parties. However, in business settings we think of attraction as a general feeling or desire that impacts our willingness to initiate and maintain a relationship with others in the organization.[36] People in business settings may be perceived as more or less attractive based on personality factors, success, or skill level. More specifically, in terms of attraction, we initiate and maintain relationships based on:

- **Task attractiveness**: The qualities that are considered appealing when the goal is to carry out workplace responsibilities. People at work seek to build relationships with others who are known for getting the job done.

- **Proximity attractiveness**: The closer our physical distance, the more likely we will build a relationship with the other party. For example, individuals with adjacent offices or work stations will have a greater opportunity to develop a relationship and will likely know more about that relational partner than those with work stations separated by a greater distance. A virtual organizational setting provides new opportunities and new limitations on how workplace relationships evolve.

- **Social attractiveness**: This type of attractiveness centers on the degree to which an individual is liked and valued by others for their social skills. In organizations, people frequently ask questions such as, "Is this a person that you could spend 40+ hours a week with?" This type of question is aimed directly at the perceived level of social attractiveness of the other party.

- **Supportive/mentoring attractiveness**: Organizations are social systems in which qualities such as empathy and helpfulness are valued. Thus, an individual's level of attraction to others is impacted by perceptions of the willingness to support others and aid in their career development.

A third dimension of relationships is known as involvement. **Involvement** refers to the amount of interaction that takes place between the relational parties. In general, more interaction tends to lead to a greater degree of self-disclosure and the perception of commitment to the other party than does less interaction. When we engage in self-disclosure with the other party, we decide to share with the other party information about ourselves that would be difficult or impossible to acquire from other sources. Disclosure signals to the other party the level of closeness that we seek in the relationship. Simply put, if I seek a closer relationship with the other party, I will tell him or her my secrets, and I expect that person to tell me his or her secrets. If I do not seek close ties in the relationship, my topics of discussion will include little, if any, personal information.

The **situation** or circumstances in which people work together will also impact the relationship that they develop. When circumstances change in the workplace, relationships will likely be affected. For example, during times of downsizing in an organization, people may be laid off or seek other employment. People in organizations accept new positions within the company, change their employment status (full-time/part-time), or are assigned different duties and responsibilities. As situations evolve, relationships wax and wane. Consider your situation in this course. As participants in this course, you have established relationships with the teacher as well as your classmates. At the end of the semester, the situation will change. You will not have a commitment to be at a location at a particular time to work with a specific set of people. As the situation changes, you and your relational partners will have to decide whether to continue to maintain existing relationships.

Dimensions of relationships are not static. That is, they change over time. Power, attraction, involvement, and situations are subject to change in relationships, and their changes will impact on the closeness or distance that we seek with our relational partners. While many feel uncomfortable with the evolving nature of relationships, change is a normal and inevitable part of workplace relationships. Skillful communicators recognize that relationships wax and wane, and adjust to new ways of defining the relationship or use communication to repair the relationship. One way of explaining how these changes take place focuses on stages of relationships. As relationships develop and communication changes with our relational partner, we deepen or weaken ties that hold the relationship together. In the following section, we discuss how relationships move through predictable phases or patterns.

The Case of the Relationship Revolution

David Jaynes, a marketing and logistics major, couldn't believe his luck. He had worked each summer in Nashville for a company that imported furniture from around the world. His summer work largely dealt with clerical and warehousing tasks, but as he approached graduation, his employer (Hillsdale House) offered him a full-time job. The group he worked with in the warehouse was happy for David and celebrated his full-time job offer with a party. David was pleasantly surprised to learn how popular he was with his co-workers.

A couple of days after the party, David arrived for his first day at work in his new role as logistics division manager. David was now a "salaried" employee and was expected to work as many hours as necessary to make sure tasks were completed. In this new role he now supervised the hourly employees he formerly worked with. From David's view this was a plus, since he would not have to worry about establishing relationships with a new group of people. His former co-workers also liked the arrangement and felt like David would work with rather than against them.

After a few days on the new job David started to notice that several of the hourly employees were taking a longer lunch hour and not clocking in or out appropriately. When he mentioned to the work crew the importance of clocking in and out according to the company rules, his former co-workers smiled and assured him that they would follow the rules in the future. However, nothing changed over the course of the next few days. David knew he was being tested but was reluctant to take on his former co-workers within a week of assuming the role of manager.

Based on your readings, how has David's relationship changed with his co-workers?

How would you resolve this situation?

Stages of Relationships

There are several models that seek to explain the stages that we follow from initiating to terminating relationships. Perhaps the most widely known model builds on the work of Mark Knapp.[37] Knapp suggests that costs and rewards are the general motivation behind the establishment of relationships. Simply put, relationships are based on an exchange. We seek to maximize rewards and minimize costs.

According to Knapp, we follow predictable phases or stages in establishing and terminating relationships. Specifically, these phases include five stages of coming together and five stages of coming apart. The stages involved in coming together begin with initiating and may eventually evolve into bonding. In contrast, when relationships begin to de-escalate or come apart we fall into the differentiating stage, and may eventually evolve into a terminating stage.

Stages of Relationships

COMING TOGETHER	COMING APART
Stage One—Initiating	Stage One—Differentiating
Stage Two—Experimenting	Stage Two—Circumscribing
Stage Three—Intensifying	Stage Three—Stagnating
Stage Four—Integrating	Stage Four—Avoiding
Stage Five—Bonding	Stage Five—Terminating

Coming together. Relationships begin with the **initiation** stage. In the initiation stage, both parties develop mutual awareness of the other party. We recognize this individual and associate him/her with some aspect of our work world. Communication associated with this stage is limited to greetings (e.g., "How are you?" followed by, "Fine. How are you?"). The relationship may remain in this stage, or it may move on to the second stage known as experimenting. In the **experimenting** stage of relationships, the parties move beyond mutual awareness and begin to engage in "small talk" or discussions of common concern (e.g., weather, state of the local economy, gas prices, etc.). One or both parties will begin to experiment at this stage by seeking out commonalities as a basis for developing a closer relationship. For example, one or both parties may explore how the other feels about company policies or events that take place at work. At this stage of the relationship, the parties have made no commitments to do things together outside of regular duties and responsibilities (e.g., eating lunch together). As with the initiation stage, a workplace relationship may remain at this stage, or it may evolve into the third stage of coming together.

In the **intensifying** stage of relationships, the parties develop a greater degree of closeness and begin to commit to activities outside of their assigned duties and responsibilities. Relational partners at this stage begin to speak of a "we," as in "we like to walk over lunch" or "we

like to be the top marketing team." In this stage, the partners disclose to a greater degree and often develop their own language based on private symbols springing from shared experiences and knowledge of each other's habits. Few relationships in organizations develop beyond this point. However, if the relationship continues to develop, the relational partners reach what is referred to as the integrating stage of a relationship.

In the **integrating** stage, the relational partners are viewed by others as having a clear identity as a duo or twosome. The relational partners are treated as a unit by co-workers and information shared with one person is expected to be shared with the other. For example, William Hewlett and David Packard, the founders of what is commonly known today as HP or Hewlett-Packard, formed a lifelong business partnership that began in the 1930s and continued until 1996, with the passing of David Packard. As reported on the HP Web site:

> Following graduation as electrical engineers from Stanford University in 1934, Bill Hewlett and Dave Packard go on a two-week camping and fishing trip in the Colorado mountains, during which they become close friends. Bill continues graduate studies at MIT and Stanford while Dave takes a job with General Electric. With the encouragement of Stanford professor and mentor Fred Terman, the two decide to start a business "and make a run for it" themselves. Hewlett-Packard Company is founded January 1, 1939.

> Dave and his wife Lucile move into the first-floor flat of a house at 367 Addison Avenue, Palo Alto, California. Bill rents the shed behind the house, and Bill and Dave begin part-time work in the garage with $538 in working capital. The $538 consists of cash and a used Sears-Roebuck drill press. http://www.hp.com/hpinfo/abouthp/histnfacts/index.html

Despite its rather modest beginnings, Hewlett-Packard is now one of the largest information technology companies in the world, with revenues in excess of $104 billion and 172,000 employees. Their relationship remained at the integrating stage throughout their professional lives. Even today it is difficult to separate their contributions to the company, since both participated in most all aspects of the life of the company, from crafting the organization's objectives to sharing leadership roles.

The final stage of relationships is known as **bonding**. Bonding suggests that the relational partners have made a public commitment to the relationship. This type of relationship is most visible in family-owned companies where relationships extend beyond the workplace. For example, organizations such as James Construction make public their committed relationships when describing the company.

James Construction Company, Inc. is a family-owned contracting business involved in site development projects. The firm was originally founded in 1937 by Alexander Potash, and is now owned and operated by third- and fourth-generation family members.

The company specializes in excavation, earth moving, grading, underground utility installation, and site concrete construction. Projects are generally contracted through construction managers for commercial, industrial, and institutional clients. Most of the project sites today are pharmaceutical and chemical facilities, but the firm has also completed many office building, hospital/medical facility, college campus, and shopping mall sites. http://www.jamesconstruction.com/

Their bonded relationships indicate a web of responsibilities and commitment between relational partners that exceed other types of relationships. Outside of family-owned businesses, relational obligations rarely extend across generations.

In sum, relationships may develop from mutual awareness to bonded ties that extend across generations. Movement through these stages is characterized by increasing amounts of communication, and that communication involves increasing levels of self-disclosure. Research makes clear that relationships do move through predictable stages, but there does not appear to be a set time that a relationship must remain in any one phase. We also know that the movement through the stages may stop at any phase from initiating to bonding. Thus, the relational partners may remain in the experimenting phase of a relationship for years, or may move from initiating to intensifying in the space of a few weeks. In addition, relationships in the workplace can begin to dissolve or come apart. In the following section we discuss the stages through which the dissolution of a relationship takes place.

Coming apart. When relationships begin to come apart, we initially begin to focus on the ways in which we differ from our relationship partner. This practice is in sharp contrast to the practice when initiating relationships and the focus on similarities. In this initial stage, referred to as **differentiating**, individuality is highlighted. For example, we may begin to point out to our relational partner differences over company policy. In this early phase of coming apart, such comments will not likely generate conflict. If this practice continues, there will be increased interest in what "I" want rather than what my relational partner wants.

In the next stage, **circumscribing**, fewer topics are raised for fear of conflict. Comments such as, "Let's not go there," are heard more often as the relationship begins to decay. Changes in topics of discussion and reluctance to discuss many issues make clear to both parties that the relationship is beginning to decay. If the relational partners do not act to repair the relationship, it will continue into the next stage, known as **stagnating**. In this stage, one or both parties invest little, if any, energy to maintain the relationship. For example, calls or emails will not receive a response, and commitments to engage in activities will wane.

If the stagnating experience continues and the relational partners begin to view the relationship as unpleasant, the stage of **avoidance** may result. In this stage, partners make excuses why they can't see or interact with one another. Increasingly, communication between the two is reduced. It is often impossible to physically avoid someone at work, but non-work-related activities such as lunch or coffee breaks will be experienced separately. One or both partners will change their work routines and will no longer be available for joint activities ("Sorry, but I have a deadline to meet so I can't have lunch.").

The **terminating** stage occurs when the partners decide, jointly or individually, to put a permanent end to the relationship. Some relationships terminate shortly after the relationship has been established, while others may terminate after longer periods as co-workers and/or friends. The termination process may be straightforward and swift ("We have to end this"), it may involve an unspoken understanding where nonverbal cues convey that the relationship is at an end, or it may take a great deal of discussion. For example, the well-publicized dispute between Michael Eisner (former CEO of Walt Disney) and Jeffrey Katzenburg resulted in Katzenburg's resignation from Disney, an extensive legal battle, and ultimately the termination of their relationship over a period of years.

Supervisory–Subordinate Relationships

While we form relationships with many different people as part of work life, few are as important as the relationship we have with our supervisor. In general, the relationship a person has with his or her supervisor is the single most important relationship a person has in the organization. A supervisor evaluates performance, makes decisions about raises and/or promotions, and is the person that subordinates seek out when in need of assistance. In fact, this relationship is the best predictor of how satisfied a subordinate is with their job, how committed they are to the company, and how satisfied they are with communication in the organization. However, the relationship takes on qualities not found in peer relationships. For example, it is acceptable for subordinates to disclose far more personal information than for supervisors. Consider your communication behavior when dealing with supervisors. You may have disclosed private information about a personal matter to a teacher as part of an explanation as to why an assignment was not completed by the due date. However, has a teacher ever pulled you aside and said, "I really need to get this off my chest. My marriage is going very badly and I'm not sure that I can complete the grading on your assignment." Simply put, it is considered unacceptable for supervisors to disclose to the same level as subordinates.

In addition to the differences in self-disclosure, the supervisory–subordinate relationship has other unique characteristics. In a series of studies, Fred Jablin and his colleagues examined the factors that impact the supervisor–subordinate relationship.[38] In the following section, we profile the characteristics associated with the "average" supervisor–subordinate relationship.

In general, between one-third and two-thirds of a supervisor's time is spent interacting with subordinates. Thus, the bulk of what most supervisors do involves communication. While the subordinate's job satisfaction is linked to how much interaction they have with their supervisor, the supervisor does not (in general) derive as much satisfaction from the relationships as subordinates. There are several reasons for this interesting finding. First, supervisors often deal with subordinates when they are presented with a problem (e.g., a piece of equipment has failed, customer complaints, problems with resources, etc.) that the subordinate is unable to solve. Second, supervisors prefer to spend time with their own boss (in general), since that person writes their performance appraisal, awards raises, and helps them with their problems. Third, supervisors and subordinates sometimes perceive events in the workplace differently. Specifically, these differences center on perceptions of openness, upward distortion, semantic information distance, and upward influence in the supervisor–subordinate relationship.

OPENNESS

Openness in the supervisory–subordinate relationship is defined as the willingness of *both* parties to be willing, receptive listeners. This is perhaps the single most important factor in the supervisory–subordinate relationship. In supervisory–subordinate relationships with a high degree of openness, subordinates are more candid in their interactions with their supervisor and more willing to reveal information that may be perceived as negative. Not surprisingly, a high degree of openness in this relationship is linked to higher levels of job satisfaction for subordinates. In relationships with a low degree of openness, subordinates are less willing to reveal negative information and report lower levels of job satisfaction.

UPWARD DISTORTION

Upward distortion is defined as subordinates intentionally distorting information in their communication with supervisors. Upward distortion occurs for several reasons. Subordinates seek to put a positive spin on the information they share with supervisors in order to manage their career and influence performance evaluations. Moreover, subordinates may have concerns about the consequences of telling the complete truth as they understand it. Upward distortion occurs in all supervisory–subordinate relationships, but is most prevalent when there is a low degree of openness between the supervisor and subordinate.

SEMANTIC INFORMATION DISTANCE

Semantic information distance refers to the gap in information and understanding that exists between supervisors and subordinates. Not surprisingly, we expect supervisors to know more than subordinates about company policies and how to carry out work-related tasks. This difference between what a supervisor knows and what his/her subordinates know has a special impact on the subordinate. Where this gap is large, subordinate job satisfaction tends to be lower. Simply put, subordinates may perceive that they do not have adequate information about the company or their job in order to function effectively. In situations where the gap is small, subordinates report higher levels of job satisfaction and a greater sense of job-related competence.

UPWARD INFLUENCE

Upward influence refers to subordinates' perceptions of how influential their supervisor is with upper management. Subordinates do take stock of which supervisors are more influential and which are less influential with upper management. In situations where a supervisor is perceived as having a great deal of influence with upper management, subordinates report higher levels of job satisfaction because they feel the supervisor is more likely to be "in the know" about the organization. Moreover, subordinates seek to strengthen ties with an upwardly influential supervisor, since any benefits awarded to the supervisor (promotion, raise, additional office space, etc.) may benefit the subordinate.

Peer Relationships

According to Modaff and DeWine, interpersonal relationships among peers in organizations can take on two forms: organizational and personal.[39] In an organizational interpersonal peer relationship, individuals come together because of assigned duties and responsibilities (e.g., similar scheduling, joint project assignment, etc.). In this situation, the relationship centers on task-oriented matters. That is, our relationship is all about our jobs. This relationship may remain focused on task-related matters or may evolve into a personal relationship (see the previous material on stages of relationships). A personal relationship may develop because of similar interests and viewpoints, as well as to meet the social and emotional needs of the relational partners. People also derive social support from personal relationships in organizations and a sense of belonging. However, peer relationships may also experience negative outcomes. For example, being awarded support from your relational partner may result in the other party perceiving they are "owed" support at a time of their choosing, even if you feel the support is unwarranted. Moreover, partners may develop a dependency on the other party and may, as a result, be unable to act independently.[40]

Sexual Harassment

Co-worker relationships follow predictable patterns. However, co-worker relationships are also capable of extremes, as in the case of sexual harassment. Why does sexual harassment occur in the workplace? O'Hair, Friedrich, and Dixon offer three reasons.[41] First, the most obvious answer is attraction. A second reason is power. That is, the harasser seeks to exert power and authority over the victim and believes that access to sex will result in ultimate relational power. Third, differences in communication styles between men and women may result in inaccurate interpretations of intent. For example, women tend to disclose more than their male counterparts, and this may be interpreted as a signal suggesting romantic interest. In reality, most women in most situations have no thought of sexual intimacy when disclosing personal information to a male colleague. Thus, there tends to be some confusion in the workplace between the sexes about what constitutes sexual harassment.

Many organizations have sought to clarify what is meant by sexual harassment through training and clear policy statements. For example, the U.S. Department of Agriculture states its position on sexual harassment:

> It is imperative that all employees in the Agricultural Research Service (ARS) are permitted to work in an environment free from unwanted sexual harassment and retaliation for reporting such harassment. Sexual harassment is an offensive working condition that will not be tolerated by this Agency.

> This policy applies to and protects every ARS employee, customer, applicant, and all ARS work sites. The intent of this policy is to ensure understanding of expectations and responsible behavior in the workplace. Conduct that may not be offensive in a social environment can be offensive at work. Sexual behavior that is repeated, unwanted, and interferes with a person's job is not only inappropriate, but also illegal, because it is a form of sex discrimination that violates Title VII of the Civil Rights Act of 1964. http://www.ars.usda.gov/aboutus/docs.htm?docid=1486

CHAPTER 9

The law regarding sexual harassment in the workplace is as follows:

Sexual Harassment

The U.S. Equal Employment Opportunity Commission is the federal agency that enforces laws pertaining to sexual harassment. The agency makes clear on its Web site what constitutes sexual harassment. The statement reads as follows:

Sexual harassment is a form of sex discrimination that violates Title VII of the Civil Rights Act of 1964. Title VII applies to employers with 15 or more employees, including state and local governments. It also applies to employment agencies and to labor organizations, as well as to the federal government.

Unwelcome sexual advances, requests for sexual favors, and other verbal or physical conduct of a sexual nature constitute sexual harassment when this conduct explicitly or implicitly affects an individual's employment, unreasonably interferes with an individual's work performance, or creates an intimidating, hostile, or offensive work environment.

Sexual harassment can occur in a variety of circumstances, including but not limited to the following:

> The victim as well as the harasser may be a woman or a man. The victim does not have to be of the opposite sex.

> The harasser can be the victim's supervisor, an agent of the employer, a supervisor in another area, a co-worker, or a non-employee.

> The victim does not have to be the person harassed but could be anyone affected by the offensive conduct.

> Unlawful sexual harassment may occur without economic injury to or discharge of the victim.

> The harasser's conduct must be unwelcome.

It is helpful for the victim to inform the harasser directly that the conduct is unwelcome and must stop. The victim should use any employer complaint mechanism or grievance system available.

http://www.eeoc.gov/types/sexual_harassment.html

A problem in overcoming sexual harassment is the tendency of the victim to avoid confronting the problem. Victims are often targeted by individuals in positions of power making it difficult to confront the harasser. Moreover, the victim may believe that revealing the harassment may backfire and lead to allegations about their motives. Finally, individuals often believe that complaints may do long-term harm to their career options in the organization.

When sexual harassment takes place, it is usually accompanied by one or more of the following signs:

- Unwelcome remarks

- Embarrassing jokes

- Taunting

- Sexist remarks

- Displays of pornographic or offensive materials and photos

Key Terms

Dimensions of relationships

Power and status

Attraction

Involvement

The situation

Stages of relationships

Coming together—stages

Coming apart—stages

Supervisory–subordinate relationships

Openness

Upward distortion

Upward influence

Semantic information distance

Peer relationships

Sexual harassment

ENDNOTES

33. Andrews, P.H., & Baird, J. (2005). *Communication for business and the professions* (8th ed.). Long Grove, IL: Waveland Press.

34. French, R., & Raven, B. (1968). Bases of Social Power. In D. Cartwright & A. Zander (Eds.), *Group dynamics* (pp. 601–623). New York: Harper & Row.

35. Frost, D., & Stahelski, A.J. (2006). The systematic measurement of French and Raven's bases of social power in workgroups. *Journal of Applied Psychology*, 18, 375–389.

36. Eichhorn, K.C., Thomas-Maddox, C., & Wanzer, M.B. (2007). *Interpersonal communication: Building rewarding relationships*. Dubuque, IA: Kendall-Hunt.

37. Knapp, M.L. (1978). *Social intercourse: From greeting to goodbye.* Boston: Allyn & Bacon.

38. For a review of this work, see

    Jablin, F., & Putnam, L. (2004). *The new handbook of organizational communication: Advances in theory, research, and methods.* Thousand Oaks, CA: Sage.

39. Modaff, D.P., & DeWine, S. (2002). *Organizational communication: Foundations, challenges, and misunderstandings.* Los Angeles: Roxbury.

40. Berlin-Ray, E. (1993). When links become chains: Considering dysfunctions of supportive communication in the workplace. *Communication Monographs, 60,* 106–111.

41. O'Hair, D., Friedrich, G., & Dixon, L. (2005). *Strategic communication in business and the professions.* Boston: Houghton-Mifflin.

CHAPTER 10

INTERCULTURAL COMMUNICATION

Overview

Diversity is an increasingly prominent part of everyday life. Regardless of where people live in the United States, they encounter others with different nationalities, religions, cultural backgrounds, and belief systems. Consider the following statistical information. In the 1970s, roughly 12% of the population was black, Hispanic, or Asian-American. According to the 2010 U.S. census, approximately 28% of the U.S. population was composed of people from these groups. One in four people in the U.S. practice a religion that falls outside of Christianity. Moreover, population trends suggested by the 2010 U.S. census indicate that Hispanics and Asian-Americans are the fastest growing groups in the country. In east Tennessee, Hispanics constitute the fastest growing segment of the population (U.S. Census, 2011).

You now live in an age when all of the people on Earth, regardless of their background or culture, are interconnected. Some of these connections may be apparent during the course of your day-to-day life when someone with an unusual accent speaks to you or you interact with someone wearing clothing that you do not associate with "mainstream" culture. Other connections may have broader implications for life in the U.S., such as the effect the "Arab Spring" has had on American political thought or the influence of English musical artists on their U.S. counterparts. More than ever, it seems that what happens in one place touches all parts of the world. As a communicator, your success depends on how you adapt and relate to other members of this global communication environment.

In Chapter Ten, you will learn about:

- What Is Considered Intercultural Communication

- Culture and How It Is Defined

- Cultural Differences in Communication

- How to Connect with Diverse Audiences

- Resources that Are Available to Strengthen Intercultural Communication

Intercultural Communication Defined

Our most significant values, beliefs, and attitudes are rooted in culture. Culture provides communicators with a lens through which they understand and interpret the world around them. While you may communicate most often with people who share your cultural understandings, you do encounter people in your classes or where you work who embrace a different cultural worldview. When communicating with someone you view as culturally different, you are experiencing intercultural communication. Intercultural communication may be defined as "interaction between two people whose cultural perceptions and symbol systems are distinct enough to alter the communication event" (Samovar, Porter, McDaniel, 2007, p. 10). The ways in which communication events are altered spring from the cultural differences that exist between people involved in the interaction.

The role of culture is the key to understanding our definition of intercultural communication. When thinking of culture, many people may think of groups that represent different national backgrounds. National cultures do exist, and they play an important role in shaping the way people communicate. However, there are many factors that define a culture and shape the way people communicate. These factors include:

- Race/ethnicity

- Nationality/geographic region

- Age

- Physical ability/disability

- Socioeconomic status

- Gender

- Language

- Religious affiliation

- Political affiliation

With these factors in mind, we will define culture as "a learned set of shared interpretations about beliefs, values, and norms which affect the behaviors of a relatively large group of people" (Lustig & Koester, 2003, p. 27).

A Truly Powerful Force

"Culture makes people understand each other better. And if they understand each other better in their soul, it is easier to overcome the economic and political barriers. But first they have to understand that their neighbour is, in the end, just like them, with the same problems, the same questions."

—Paulo Coelho, Brazilian lyricist and author most widely known for his work *The Alchemist*

It is important to understand that culture is learned—it is not innate. By this we mean culture is not a quality that people possess at birth. For example, there is no preexisting cultural identity for Koreans or Jordanians or Canadians. People begin to acquire knowledge of the culture they were born into soon after birth. When a person achieves competence in a particular culture, he or she has become enculturated. As a result of being born into U.S. culture, you began at an early age to think and act differently than people born in Poland or Nigeria or New Zealand. Interestingly, these ways of thinking and acting tend to be taken for granted. Cultures are invisible to the people used to inhabiting them. But for people from different cultures, it is obvious that culture exerts enormous influence in how people live and communicate with one another.

One final consideration we wish you to consider about culture: Simply put, we cannot say that one culture is superior to all other cultures. As communicators, we can (and should!) recognize that other cultures exist and adapt our messages accordingly. However, operating from the view that "my" culture is superior to others is often the root cause of conflict between peoples embracing different cultural perspectives. Too often a superficial knowledge of other cultures tends to breed negative judgments when cultural differences come into view. The kind of negative evaluation that is sometimes assigned to a different culture is illustrated well by a quote from the ancient Greek playwright Aeschylus who wrote over two thousand years ago, "Everyone is quick to blame the alien" (Kerrigan, 1998).

The experience of intercultural communication can be uncomfortable for some. Understanding and appreciating cultural differences, separating important cultural differences from those that are inconsequential, and interpreting messages as intended by the sender present very real challenges to effective communication. One useful practice to follow when seeking to understand people from different cultures is to learn about their proverbs. Proverbs communicate the widespread beliefs and values of people from a particular culture. For example, in the U.S. it is common to say that "actions speak louder than words." Americans embrace a "doing" culture and getting things done is highly valued in the U.S. Interestingly, as the following concepts suggest, people across the globe share many ideas but may express them differently:

- **Sweep only in front of your own door.** This German proverb reflects the very private nature of the Germans and their strong dislike of gossip. There is a somewhat similar proverb found in Swedish culture: *He who stirs another's porridge often burns his own.*

- **A zebra does not despise its stripes.** From the Maasai of Africa, this saying expresses the value of accepting things as they are. There is a similar proverb found in the Mexican culture: *I dance to the tune that is played.*

CHAPTER 10

- **A man's tongue is his sword.** With this saying Arabs are taught to value words and use them in a powerful and forceful manner.

- **Those who know do not speak and those who speak do not know.** This famous doctrine, in the *Analects* of Confucius, stressing silence over talk is very different from the advice given in the previous Arab proverb.

- **When spider webs unite they can tie up a lion.** This Ethiopian proverb teaches the importance of collectivism and group solidarity. In the Japanese culture the same idea is expressed with the following proverb: *A single arrow is easily broken, but not in a bunch.* For the Yoruba of Africa, the same lesson is taught with the proverb that notes: *A single hand cannot lift the calabash to the head.*

Cultural Differences and Communication

Cultural differences impact how people deliver presentations as well as how they respond to presentations. Some differences are more impactful than others, and in the following section we will examine many of the features of culture that have the potential to influence the success of your presentations.

1. **Formality.** During the course of a presentation, the speaker seeks to establish a relationship with the members of the audience. People in the U.S. often seek to establish informal relationships with audience members. For example, first names are often used when referring to self or others as a way of indicating friendliness and inclusiveness. However, in other cultures (e.g., German culture) it is generally considered inappropriate to adopt an informal presentation style.

Zhè shì wǒde míngpiàn.
這 是 我的 名片。
'This is my business card.'

©Hayden-McNeil, LLC

2. **Social customs.** Most all cultures have established traditions or customs for speaking events. To the members of the culture, customs provide guidelines for what is appropriate in a public speaking setting. Not surprisingly, those not enculturated into a particular culture may have difficulty determining what is happening. For example, at the conclusion of a speech delivered in Ulm, Germany, the speaker from the U.S. was surprised by the reaction of the audience. Audience members did not clap at the conclusion of the speech. Rather, they lightly struck the tables they were seated at for approximately two minutes. According to custom, applause in Germany takes the form of lightly striking a table or other solid object rather than clapping hands.

3. **Dress.** Professional or business attire is the norm for speakers outside the U.S. Wearing the latest fashion or the traditional college uniform (i.e., jeans and t-shirts) as is often the case in the U.S. would be viewed as inappropriate in most cultures across the globe.

4. **Gender.** Conceptions of gender-related appropriateness in public speaking or presentation contexts vary considerably across cultures. In many cultures, women are restricted in terms of how they may participate as a speaker or as a member of the audience. Such restrictions are not limited to different cultures outside the U.S. Within the U.S., some cultural groups do place restrictions on when women may speak or how they may participate as members of the audience.

5. **Time.** In general, time is viewed in one of two ways across cultures. First, in many cultures (such as here in the U.S.) time is viewed in monochromic terms. That is, time is seen as something that is almost tangible—it is something that can be scheduled and tasks are arranged for designated times. Language use in the U.S. also reflects this view. In this culture we do not like to waste time, and we set aside time for others. Second, a polychromic view of time places more importance on relationships in communication events than on the role of time. In cultures such as Greece or Mexico, you establish or renew relationships before engaging in presentation events. Thus, in some cultures speaking on time and not going over the assigned time is essential; in other cultures maintaining the speaking schedule is subordinate to relational factors.

CHAPTER 10

The kinds of differences described can present challenges when you are preparing and delivering presentations. The table below summarizes how cultural characteristics influence public speaking and presentations in three separate cultures.

Cultural Characteristics and Public Speaking/Presentations

	U.S.	JAPAN	MEXICO
Social unit	Individual	Group	Family
Authority relationships	Egalitarian	Hierarchical	Hierarchical
Basis for authority	Competence	Seniority	Trust
Attitude toward competition	Seeks	Avoids	Avoids
Importance of relationships	Helpful	Essential	Essential
Basis for status	Money/ competence	Title/ position	Title/ position
Role of formality	Medium	High	High
Sense of history	Low	High	High
Importance of time	High	High	Low

Connecting with Intercultural Audiences

Speakers can encounter a wide range of difficulties when dealing with a diverse audience, but these challenges can be dealt with if you follow a few commonsense guidelines. According to Morreale (2010) there are three practices you can follow to avoid problems speaking with interculturally diverse audiences.

First, stay up-to-date with current events and trends. What is meant by Arab Spring? How are social movements being influenced by social networking Web sites? How is immigration discussed in the presidential campaign? When a speaker uses terms that are out of date or uses inappropriate terms that have recently gained wide public circulation, the audience will rightly assume the speaker is out of touch.

Second, don't add irrelevant identifiers and/or associations. Avoid making statements that include identifiers such as the female officer, the male nurse, or the Arab-American scientist. Does it matter that the nurse is a male? Would it matter if the nurse was French? In most all cases, the answer is no. These kinds of identifiers are often worse than useless: they have the potential to focus audience attention on irrelevant qualities. Audience members may also wonder if the use of the identifiers and associations is strategic. That is, they may suspect that you were using identifiers for some purpose other than the surface level goal.

Third, avoid using stereotypical information in speeches. Even well-intentioned people can make use of stereotypes that produce negative perceptions in audience members. Whether it's conveying the idea that all Southerners like country music or that student athletes are not concerned about their grades, the problem is generalizing limited and inaccurate perceptions of a few people to all members of the group, race, or gender.

International/Intercultural Online Resources

SCHOLARLY RESOURCES
International Communication Association
http://www.icahdq.org/

International Communication Gazette
http://gaz.sagepub.com/

International Journal of Communication
http://ijoc.org/ojs/index.php/ijoc

International Association for Media and Communication Research
http://iamcr.org/

FACT BOOKS
CIA World Factbook
https://www.cia.gov/library/publications/the-world-factbook/

Internet Library for Librarians
http://www.itcompany.com/inforetriever/almanac.htm

PRESENTATION RESOURCES
Gifts of Speeches
http://gos.sbc.edu/

Great Speeches of the 20th Century
http://www.guardian.co.uk/theguardian/series/greatspeeches

UN Women
http://www.unwomen.org/category/speeches/

Speeches of Tony Blair
http://www.tonyblairoffice.org/speeches/

TED—Ideas Worth Spreading
http://www.ted.com/

TED—100 Websites to Know and Use
http://blog.ted.com/2007/08/03/100_websites_yo/

CHAPTER 10

ENDNOTES

42. Kerrigan, J. (1998). *Revenge tragedy: Aeschylus to Armageddon.* New York: Oxford University Press.

43. Lustig, M.W., & Koester, J. (2003). *Intercultural competence: Interpersonal communication across cultures,* 4th ed. Boston: Allyn & Bacon.

44. Morreale, S.P. (2010). *The Competent Public Speaker.* New York: Peter Lang, Inc.

45. U.S. Census (2011). United States Census 2010: It's in your hands. Retrieved from http://2010.census.gov/2010census/

CHAPTER 11

COMMUNICATING IN TEAMS AND GROUPS

Overview

Teams and groups have become a regular part of the workplace. People are often organized into teams at work based on the belief that duties and responsibilities can be carried out more efficiently in a group rather than separately. Moreover, people derive social needs from group membership. While the composition of teams may vary across organizations, a team or group is composed of three or more individuals who meet regularly to work on a common goal. Each member of the group normally has a stake in the outcomes associated with the common goal.[46] In addition to sharing common objectives, groups or teams also share a number of characteristics that impact how they perform. Specifically, these characteristics include norms, pressure for uniformity, roles, cohesiveness, and coalition formation.

Group Norms

Norms are defined as the informal rules established by group members that guide the way people interact and behave.[47] In order for groups to function, norms have to be agreed upon. For example, how are we expected to divide up the workload? How often will we meet? What is the preferred way of contacting each other? The way the team decides to answer these questions contributes to the expectations and behavioral patterns that will be followed and that will aid or harm the group's ability to achieve its objectives. While norms are often formalized in manuals or on other business documents, they are frequently informal understandings that have no official standing. Are you unclear what this means? Consider the following:

> You have attended this course (Comm Studies 240) for several weeks. After the first few class sessions, you have established a pattern of sitting at the same desk in the vicinity of the same

**In Chapter Eleven,
you will learn about:**

- Communicating in Teams and Groups

- Group Dynamics—Norms, Pressure for Uniformity, Roles, Coalition Formation

- Communication and Leadership

- Effective Communication in the Group

people. The professor has established a pattern for conducting the class that you have come to expect. At this point in the semester, when you walk into class you and your classmates have a shared understanding of how the group (the class) will operate.

Now, imagine that the next time the class meets the professor assigns a new seating arrangement (you will be seated alphabetically). In addition, you (yes you!) will be expected to teach the class that day. Most likely you will be questioning this new arrangement, since it is far from the normal routine. Your questioning will likely not involve any policies that have been written into the syllabus or any other class document. Rather, you would likely question why the informal understandings and expectations (i.e., group norms) that have developed over the first few class sessions have been altered.

From the time that the team is created, group members begin to engage in the process of establishing norms. As norms come to be established, group members will also establish expectations about the extent to which members must conform to the norms. Norms may be tightly or loosely held by members of the group. The more tightly group norms are held by members, the greater the sanctions or consequences that team members will experience for violating a norm. Group norms do evolve over time as a result of situational factors or because of changes in the membership of the group. When changes in membership take place, one of the most important tasks confronting the new member is to learn the norms by which the group operates.

PRESSURE FOR UNIFORMITY

Pressure for uniformity refers to the degree to which individuals are expected to conform to group member expectations. While people often suggest that they are independent and act according to their own beliefs and values, groups in business settings do create expectations. In fact, all groups pressure members to conform to expectations to some degree. In groups with a high degree of pressure for uniformity, sanctions from other group members are imposed quickly and potentially severely on individuals for not meeting expectations. When pressure for uniformity is relatively weak, group members receive fewer sanctions for not conforming. A benefit groups derive from pressure to be uniform is that the group may be more likely to maintain itself over time. However, groups that exert strong pressure on individuals to conform may experience difficulties adapting to changing circumstances that conflict with the expectation to be uniform.

ROLES

Roles refer to the kinds of positions that people enact in groups. All group members take on roles, and often group members take on more than one role. The communication roles that group members take on are often not assigned, and it is less relevant who enacts them than that they are enacted. When group roles are not carried out, it will be difficult or impossible for the group to complete its objectives. The roles that members take on fall into two broad categories: group task roles and group maintenance and building roles. **Group task roles** involve the kinds of roles that are necessary for the group to function and facilitate goal attainment. While a wide variety of group task roles have been identified, for the purpose of this course we will review the roles that most directly involve communication. Specifically, these roles include:[48]

- **Information agent**. When a person enacts this role, he/she offers facts, beliefs, personal experience, and other inputs in order to facilitate tasks. In addition, a person in this role will ask for input from others and ask questions concerning the ideas or opinions that have been shared.

- **Elaborator**. When a person enacts this role, he/she summarizes or adds to information that has been presented to the group.

- **Initiator**. When a person enacts this role, he/she begins the process of getting the group started on their collective task.

- **Administrator**. When a person enacts this role, he/she keeps the group activities on track and is aware of time constraints.

- **Gatekeeper**. When a person enacts this role, he/she manages communication channels and will allow or restrict the flow of information between group members.

The second kind of role that people enact in groups is known as **group maintenance and building roles**. These roles involve the building and maintaining of interpersonal relationships within the group. Examples of these roles include:

- **Harmonizer**. A person enacting this role seeks to maintain good will among group members by smoothing over differences.

- **Sensor**. A person enacting this role seeks to take the emotional "pulse" of group members so as to determine moods or feelings that may impact the group's ability to maintain relationships.

- **Negotiator**. A person enacts this role when seeking to balance the needs or positions of group members.

In addition to these roles that support effective relationships, group members can take on roles that will bring about ineffective relationships. Roles such as **blocker**, **avoider**, or **recognition seeker** are enacted when individuals pursue personal rather than group objectives with behaviors that are irrelevant to the group's task. A blocker is consistently negative and continues to pursue ideas that the group has rejected. In contrast, an avoider pursues individual goals through pouting or cynicism. Finally, the recognition seeker seeks attention and consistently points to his or her achievements. In each role, the member has little interest in the group's goals or is simply not a competent communicator.

COHESIVENESS
Cohesiveness refers to the group's ability to maintain itself over time. Group cohesiveness is the product of several factors. First, participants may maintain membership in the group if they receive benefits. Second,

members may have made an investment in the group (e.g., time, resources, energy, etc.) that they do not wish to abandon. Third, members retain membership because they are committed to the goals pursued by the group. Groups that experience high levels of cohesiveness are more likely to experience a number of positive outcomes, including:

- More effective communication than in less cohesive groups.

- More influence on the task-related behaviors than in less cohesive groups.

- More effective at achieving group goals than less cohesive groups.

- More reports of satisfaction by group members than in less cohesive groups.[49]

Maintaining cohesiveness is essential to the group's success. Simply put, groups that are unable to maintain themselves tend not to achieve objectives. However, very high levels of group cohesiveness may prove to be problematic for groups. The reason is that very high levels of cohesion may lead to groupthink. **Groupthink** occurs when members of a group or team place a higher value on harmony and maintaining personal relationships than on achieving group goals.[50] People are often tempted to go along with other group members so as to maintain the benefits of group membership. To be effective, groups need to balance the competing needs of goal attainment and personal relationships.

COALITION FORMATION
Coalition formation involves the building of alliances by a subset of the group. Coalitions within the group form as the result of common interests or shared goals and tend to be temporary in nature. Forming a coalition allows the members of the alliance a greater opportunity to advance their goals within the group than if they pursued goals individually. Thus, if three members of a group that includes twelve people seek a common objective, they may form an alliance or partnership to advance that goal. However, each member of this coalition may go on to participate at a later date in other coalitions to advance different goals. Thus, the forming of coalitions within groups is a dynamic process in which alliances form, disintegrate, and reform.

Competence in building coalitions within groups is a valuable skill to possess. It is far easier to influence decisions or policies when part of a coalition than to pursue goals individually. According to research, building a successful coalition involves a series of steps.[51] Initially, individuals within the group seeking to form a coalition should focus on identifying who in the group shares mutual interests. The individuals sharing mutual interests may be readily apparent, or potential coalition members must be persuaded that forming a coalition would be to their benefit. Members are more easily persuaded to form coalitions when the case can be made that:

- Your goals are similar and compatible.

- Working together will enhance each parties' abilities to obtain their goals.

- The benefits of forming an alliance will be greater than the costs.

Deciding whether to join a coalition is both a rational and relational decision. Rationally, a group member must consider whether their goals would be helped or harmed by participation in a coalition. Relationally, a group member must consider the state of their relationship with the other party or parties and ask how likely it is that the members of the coalition can work together to achieve common objectives. When the goals of two or more people are compatible, forming a coalition will benefit all the members of the alliance.

Leadership

Leadership is important in groups. Seldom does a group or team perform well unless someone in the group steps forward to coordinate and direct its activities. **Leadership** is defined as the process of influencing group activities toward goal achievement.[52] Leadership is not interchangeable with managing. For example, a teacher possessing legitimate authority may assign you and several others to a group for an assignment, but the leader of the group acts to influence and motivate the group to achieve a particular level of performance.

Based on our definition of leadership, it is clear that all individuals are capable of taking on leadership roles in work groups. Studies of leadership have been wide-ranging, seeking answers to questions about how people come to be effective leaders. Research has explored internal qualities or traits of leaders (e.g., charisma, adaptiveness, etc.), behaviors of leaders (task-oriented vs. people-oriented), the leader's vision for the group, and the influence of the leader on the values and beliefs of followers. One constant in the studies involving leadership involves communication.

Leaders must communicate effectively, but there is no single way of communicating that will always bring about the desired results. While no one way is effective, several communication practices are consistently linked to effective leadership in groups.[53] These practices include:

- **Listening skills**. Communicating a willingness to consider the views of others.

- **Building trust**. Communicating a commitment to the group and its goals.

- **Promoting understanding**. Communicating that others' views and feelings are understood.

- **Empowering others**. Communicating that others have the opportunity to think and act for themselves.

Effective Group Communication

Groups or teams are not equally effective. So, what are the characteristics that separate groups that interact effectively from those that do not? According to Wageman, seven features separate effective groups from ineffective groups.[54]

- **Clear and engaging direction**. Group members have a clear understanding of the group's goals and strong determination to achieve the objectives.

- **The assigned work is designed to be done by a team**. The nature of the tasks requires that more than one person is needed to achieve the objective.

- **Team rewards are strongly associated with team effort**. If a team is to work well together, there must be rewards for team rather than individual efforts.

- **Physical resources are readily available**. Information, meeting space, and other relevant resources must be present in order to complete the work.

- **The team, not the leader, has the authority to make decisions over basic work strategies**. If a team is to perform at a high level, the group must feel it has the power to make decisions about how the work is to be done.

- **The team must articulate clear, measureable goals that are compatible with the organization's goals**. Without clear goals, the group's efforts will lack direction.

- **The team establishes norms that promote strategic thinking**. The group needs to set norms that allow it to think ahead about how to achieve goals in future work environments.

Key Terms

Group norms

Pressure for uniformity

Roles

Group task roles

Group maintenance and building roles

Blocker

Avoider

Recognition seeker

Cohesiveness

Groupthink

Coalition formation

Leadership

ENDNOTES

46. Putnam, L. (2003). Rethinking the nature of groups: A bona fide group perspective. In R. Hirokawa, R. Cathcart, L. Samovar, & L. Henman (eds.). *Small group communication theory and practice: An anthology* (8th ed.; pp. 8–16). Los Angeles: Roxbury Publishing.

47. Modaff, D.P., & DeWine, S. (2002). *Organizational communication: Foundations, challenges, and misunderstandings.* Los Angeles: Roxbury.

48. O'Hair, D., Friedrich, G., & Dixon, L. (2005). *Strategic communication in business and the professions.* Boston: Houghton-Mifflin Co.

49. Hirokawa, R, Cathcart, R., Samovar, L., & Henman, L. (2003). *Small group communication theory and practice: An anthology* (8th ed.). Los Angeles: Roxbury Publishing.

50. Neher, W. (1997). *Organizational communication: Challenges of change, diversity, and continuity.* Boston: Allyn and Bacon.

51. Hirokawa, R, Cathcart, R., Samovar, L., & Henman, L. (2003). *Small group communication theory and practice: An anthology* (8th ed.). Los Angeles: Roxbury Publishing.

52. Gouran, D. (2003). Leadership as the art of counteractive influence in decision-making and problem-solving groups. In R. Hirokawa, R. Cathcart, L. Samovar, & L. Henman (eds.). *Small group communication theory and practice: An anthology* (8th ed.; pp. 172–183). Los Angeles: Roxbury Publishing.

53. O'Hair, D., Friedrich, G., & Dixon, L. (2005). *Strategic communication in business and the professions.* Boston: Houghton-Mifflin Co.

54. Wageman, R. (1997). Critical success factors for creating superb self-managing teams. *Organizational Dynamics, 53,* 49–60.

CHAPTER 11

CHAPTER 12

GROUP DECISION MAKING AND PROBLEM SOLVING

Overview

One of the most important tasks that a group deals with involves decision making. Group decision making is among the most important kinds of tasks that groups undertake. Many researchers point to the quality of communication as the single biggest influence on the quality of a group's decision making.[55] Communication serves as the one process by which individual and group goals can be negotiated. The focus on communication in group decision making has emphasized the process that the group goes through to make decisions. If the process is flawed, then the decision is likely to be flawed. If the process is effective, the decision is more likely to be a good one.

According to Gouran and Hirokawa, communication during the decision-making process directly affects the critical thinking of group members. The way in which the group talks about issues affects the way they think about the issues, which in turn affects the quality of the choices they make as a group. That effect is felt in four areas where the group considers key aspects of the decision:

- Is there something about the status quo that requires improvement or change?

- What do we want to achieve or accomplish?

- What are the choices available to us?

- What are the positive and negative aspects of those choices?

In Chapter Twelve, you will learn about:

- Group Decision Making

- Patterns of Group Communication and Decision Making

- Barriers to Effective Decision Making

- Group Conflict

Patterns of Group Decision Making

When group members come together to make decisions, research suggests that they follow predictable patterns. Similar to the notion that relationships move through predictable patterns or phases, groups also follow patterns when engaged in decision making. The patterns involve both task-related activities as well as relationship negotiation. That pattern includes:[56]

- **Orientation**. During this phase, the group receives its charge (the decision-making task) from the group or team manager. During this phase, members of the group will also work on building (if not acquainted) or maintaining work relationships.

- **Conflict**. During this phase, group members begin to express competing opinions on how to proceed. The conflict phase can be productive if group members are willing to consider competing views on how to address the question. By considering all competing views, the group will have available to it the entire pool of group member ideas. Moreover, soliciting and considering competing views from group members has the advantage of strengthening group member relationships, since all members were given a chance to be heard.

- **Emergence**. During this phase, the group begins to coalesce or unite around a position. Competing views will begin to be set aside for the agreed-upon position.

- **Reinforcement**. In this phase, group members reinforce or bolster each other in the view that the position taken was the best solution to the decision despite any potential drawbacks. This process of reinforcement was captured well by Benjamin Franklin, when asked to comment on the group decision regarding the U.S. Constitution:

  > I doubt too whether any other Convention we can obtain, may be able to make a better Constitution: For when you assemble a Number of Men to have the Advantage of their joint Wisdom, you inevitably assemble with those Men all their Prejudices, their Passions, their Errors of Opinion, their local Interests, and their selfish Views. From such an Assembly can a perfect Production be expected? It therefore astonishes me, Sir, to find this System approaching so near to Perfection as it does… Thus I consent, Sir, to this Constitution because I expect no better, and because I am not sure that it is not the best.

Barriers

When group members pool their ideas, the decision of the group should result in a higher quality outcome than can be achieved by a single individual. However, group members do not always communicate in a way that allows for all members to share ideas. Some of the most common ways that group members seek to restrict the choices of the group refer to **blocking behaviors**. For the purposes of this course, we will review four kinds of blocking behaviors.[57]

- **Hidden agendas**. When a group member pursues a hidden agenda, he/she has an ulterior motive or unstated purpose for their actions. For example, a member may skew information so as to better support his/her views. In such a situation, communication is used to mask the actual goal.

- **Pulling rank**. This type of blocking behavior occurs when a group member uses legitimate authority to influence the team's decision. They may do this explicitly by making statements such as, "I will not approve of that decision." In addition, those with ranking authority may make use of implicit or unspoken ways of communicating disapproval through the use of nonverbal behaviors or facial expressions.

- **Interrupting**. This type of blocking behavior distracts group members from the topic being discussed and directs attention to other topics. Moreover, interrupting others is a subtle way of communicating that their ideas are of questionable value.

- **Defensive communication**. A variety of defensive behaviors are used as blocking behaviors. Defensive communication may involve reacting angrily to a comment, withdrawing, or making clear that the group member is unwilling to communicate further on the topic. Other group members should not allow this type of behavior to direct the team's discussions.

One way to deal effectively with the phases of decision-making and control-blocking behaviors is through the use of group **decision-making rules**. Decision-making rules make clear the "laws" or regulations members of the group are expected to follow. Determining the rules that the group will follow in the decision-making process is an activity that is separate from the actual decision making. Group decision-making rules that facilitate each phase of the process allow for contributions from all members and make blocking behaviors problematic. For example, calling on or encouraging each person to share his or her views and limiting the time any one person has to communicate will more likely lead to the pooling of all members' ideas. A cautionary note about decision-making rules: the person(s) controlling the rules will greatly influence the decision made by the group. If the group does not address the issue of decision-making rules, members will seek to bring about informal rules (including the use of blocking behaviors) to advance their personal interests. As you progress through your career, make certain that you attend closely to how the decision-making rules are determined. Simply put, the person who controls the rules controls the outcome.

Group Conflict

Conflict is a normal part of life in any work group. Conflict in groups can range from relatively mild to persistent warlike behaviors on the part of group members. From a communication perspective, **conflict** may be defined as the expressed struggle between at least two inter-dependent parties who perceive incompatible goals, scarce rewards, and interference from the other party in achieving their objectives.[58] The elements of this definition not only make clear what conflict is but offer directions on how conflict may be addressed.

- **Expressed struggle**. Conflict occurs when the parties are aware of it. Thus, if I'm mad at you but you are unaware of my feelings, we are not in conflict.

- **Two interdependent parties**. Conflict involves at least two parties that are in some way dependent on each other.

- **Perceived incompatible goals**. Conflict occurs when I believe that I can't achieve my goal if you achieve your goal.

- **Scarce rewards**. Conflict involves the distribution of scarce re-wards (financial, status, etc.).

- **Interference from the other party**. Conflict occurs when I have identified a party that is blocking my path to the goal. It's not the unknown "they" blocking my path; it's a specific party.

Conflict can have positive consequences as well as negative con-sequences. Conflict can clarify what group members value, and by working through the conflict, the group may be strengthened and better able to deal with future conflicts. Unfortunately, conflict often results in the disintegration of a group. So, how do group members manage conflicts? Research suggests two forms of conflict resolution: distributive and integrative.[59] **Distributive conflict** promotes the use of negative behaviors to prevent others from reaching their goals. More simply, this form results in goals and scarce rewards being distributed to one party. The other party does not acquire rewards or achieve objectives. In contrast, **integrative conflict** fosters cooperation and shared rewards. With integrative conflict, both parties modify their perception of incompatible goals and seek a mutually acceptable outcome. Five conflict styles are associated with these two forms of conflict resolution.[60] The five styles include:

- **Avoidance**. The most widely adopted style for dealing with conflict. When using this style, a group member will not speak up so as to avoid further conflict. This style will likely lead to a distributive conflict.

- **Accommodation**. A highly cooperative approach that is used when relationships are more important to the group members than perceived incompatible goals and scarce rewards.

- **Competition**. This method is highly aggressive and results in group members doing whatever they need to do to "win" the conflict.

- **Collaboration**. This method seeks to meet the needs of all parties and explore how perceptions of goals and rewards may be changed.

- **Compromise**. Each party comes away from the conflict with some measure of resources and/or goals.

When thinking about the conflict style that you should adopt in the group, keep in mind that situational factors will influence what is appropriate to adopt. For example, is it reasonable to pursue all possible conflicts? (Hint: Pick your battles.) In some cases, avoidance may be best if other conflicts are anticipated. As a general rule, collaboration results in the most positive outcomes. The drawback to this style is that all parties must agree to its use.

Key Terms

Patterns of group decision making

Orientation

Conflict

Emergence

Reinforcement

Blocking behaviors

Decision-making rules

Group conflict

Elements of conflict

Distributive conflict

Integrative conflict

Conflict styles

ENDNOTES

55. Keyton, J. (1999). Analyzing interaction patterns in dysfunctional teams. *Small Group Research, 30,* 364–392.

56. Hirokawa, R, Cathcart, R., Samovar, L., & Henman, L. (2003). *Small group communication theory and practice: An anthology* (8th ed.). Los Angeles: Roxbury Publishing.

57. Dodd, C.H. (2004). *Managing business and professional communication.* Boston: Allyn & Bacon.

58. Wilmot, W., & Hocker, J. (2001). *Interpersonal conflict* (6th ed.). New York: McGraw-Hill.

59. Van Slyke, E.J. (1999). *Listening to conflict: Finding constructive solutions to workplace disputes.* New York: AMACOM.

60. Wilmot, W., & Hocker, J. (2001). *Interpersonal conflict* (6th ed.). New York: McGraw-Hill.

INDEX

I

identifiers, irrelevant, 146–147
identity management objectives, 17–18
illustrations, 83
impromptu presentations, xi, 89
information agent, 151
informative presentations, xi, 97–99
initiator, 151
integrative conflict, 160
intention, 15–16
intercultural communication, 122, 142–147
interference, 19–20
internal previews, 77
internal summaries, 77
interrupting, 159
interview project, xii
interviews
  body of, 58
  closings, 59
  defined, 47
  disciplinary interviews, 61
  employment interviews, 59, 61
  establishing rapport, 57–58
  goals for, 50
  interview preview, 58
  mediated interviews, 49–50
  opening of, 57–58
  performance interviews, 61
  preparation for, 50–51
  as a process, 47
  purpose and, 48
  questions and, 48–49, 52–57
  recruitment process, 59–60
  sample questions, 62–63
  selection interview, 59
  strategies for, 51–52
  tips for, 61
  as transactions, 47
  two parties in, 48
  types of, 59–61
introduction presentations, 115
introductions, 78–79, 106, 116
invalid analogy, 111

J

Jablin, Fred, 134
James Construction Company, Inc., 132–133
jargon, 22, 98
job search process, 60
Jobs, Steven, 34

K

Katzenburg, Jeffrey, 134
Kennedy, A.A., 40
Knapp, Mark, 131
Kurtz, Howard, 5

L

landline telephones, 8
language
  appropriate use of, 121–122
  comparisons and, 123
  concrete language, 122
  meaning and, 121
  rhythmic devices, 123
  rules and, 21, 119–121
  symbols and, 120–121
  vivid language, 112, 114, 116, 122–123
leadership, 38–39, 153
  See also management
leading questions, 53–54
legitimate power, 128
line graphs, 83
linear model, 19–20
listening, 22–24
loaded questions, 54
location. *See* setting
logical fallacies, 111–112

M

main points, 67, 73, 76–77
management
  bureaucratic model, 33–35
  charismatic authority, 33–34
  classical organization theory, 32–35, 36, 39
  culture and, 40–41
  Human Relations movement, 36–37
  Human Resources approach, 37–39
  organizational charts, 34–35
  scientific management, 32–33
Maslow, Abraham, 38
Mayo, Elton, 36
McGregor, D., 39
mediated interviews, 49–50
message, 19
message factors, 107–108
metaphors, 123
mistaken cause reasoning, 111
mobile phones, 8
Modaff, D.P., 136
models, 83
moderately scheduled interviews, 51
monochromic time, 145
Monroe's Motivational Sequence, 103, 104–105, 109
Morreale, S.P., 146
motivation, 38

N

NCA ethical credo, 10
needs, 38
negotiator, 151
nervousness. *See* speech anxiety
neutral questions, 53–54
newspaper industry, 5, 8
nondirective interview strategy, 51
nonscheduled interviews, 51
nonverbal cues, 50, 54, 72, 93–94, 112
norms, group, 149–150, 154

O

O'Hair, D., 137
O'Keefe, D.J., 100
open-ended questions, 52–53
openness, 135
organizational charts, 34–35
organizational patterns, 73–75, 76, 101–105
organizations
  bureaucratic model, 33–35
  charismatic authority, 33–34
  classical organization theory, 32–35, 36, 39
  communication and, 31–32, 39
  culture and, 40–41
  Human Relations movement, 36–37
  Human Resources approach, 37–39
  organizational charts, 34–35
  precedent and usage, 34
  scientific management, 32–33
orientation, 158
outlines, 80–81

P

parallelism, 123
pauses, 92, 112
PepsiCo, 6
performance interviews, 61
personal appearance, xiv, 17, 24, 25–26, 94
persuasion
  defined, 99–100
  target audience attitude change model, 100–101
persuasive presentations
  emotional appeals and, 112–113
  fear appeals and, 108
  guidelines for, xi
  logical fallacies and, 111–112
  message factors, 107–108
  Monroe's Motivational Sequence, 103, 104–105, 109
  questions of fact, 101–102
  questions of policy, 103–104, 109
  questions of value, 102–103